W9-AMS-614

For current pricing information,
or to learn more about this or any Nextext title,
call us toll-free at **1-800-323-5435**
or visit our web site at www.nextext.com.

A LITERARY READER

Women's
VOICES

nextext

Compiled by: Pamela Harkins, Northwestern University, Evanston, Illinois, and Karen Leick, Northwestern University, Evanston, Illinois.

Cover photograph: Virginia Woolf, ©Hulton-Deutsch Collection/CORBIS

Printed in the United States of America

ISBN 0-618-04817-0

1 2 3 4 5 6 7 — QKT — 06 05 04 03 02 01 00

Table of Contents

*Throughout the reader, vocabulary words appear in boldface
type and are footnoted. Specialized or technical words and phrases
appear in lightface type and are footnoted.*

Growing Up
Female

What the Good Man Does Is Always Right

BY HANS CHRISTIAN ANDERSEN

Hans Christian Andersen (1805–1875) was born in Odense, Denmark. He is most well known for his fairy tales, although he is also the author of plays, novels, poems, travel books, and several autobiographies. Andersen's fairy tales first appeared in Danish in the 1830s and 1840s but have now been translated throughout the world, making them some of the most frequently translated works in all literary history. This story cleverly introduces a moral that any reader will recognize as faulty. Andersen's tale, so frequently read by children all over the world, might be seen to reinforce gender stereotypes. But the absurdity of the tale turns this message on its head.

I will tell you a story which was told to me when I was a little boy. Every time I thought of the story, it seemed to me to become more and more charming, for it is with stories as it is with many people—they become better as they grow older.

I take it for granted that you have been in the country and seen a very old farmhouse with a thatched roof, and mosses and small plants growing wild upon the thatch.[1] There is a stork's nest on the summit of the gable;[2] for we can't do without the stork. The walls of the house are sloping and the windows are low, and only one of the latter is made so that it will open. The baking oven sticks out of the wall like a little fat body. The elder tree hangs over the paling,[3] and beneath its branches, at the foot of the paling, is a pool of water in which a few ducks are disporting[4] themselves. There is a yard dog too, who barks at all comers.

Just such a farmhouse stood out in the country, and in this house dwelt an old couple—a peasant and his wife. Small as was their property, there was one article among it that they could do without—a horse, which made a living out of the grass it found by the side of the highroad. The old peasant rode into the town on this horse, and often his neighbors borrowed it of him and rendered the old couple some service in return for the loan of it. But they thought it would be best if they sold the horse or exchanged it for something that might be more useful to them. But what might this *something* be?

"You'll know that best, old man," said the wife. "It is fair day[5] today, so ride into town and get rid of the horse for money, or make a good exchange. Whichever you do will be right to me. Ride off to the fair."

And she fastened his neckerchief for him, for she could do that better than he could. And she tied it in a double bow, for she could do that very prettily. Then she

---

[1] thatch—straw, reeds, or similar material used to cover a roof.

[2] gable—triangular end of a building under the structure of the roof.

[3] paling—picket fence.

[4] disporting—amusing.

[5] fair day—the day a local fair is held in town. People would come to the fair to buy and sell goods and enjoy games, entertainment, and food.

brushed his hat round and round with the palm of her hand, and gave him a kiss. So he rode away upon the horse that was to be sold or to be **bartered**[6] for something else. Yes, the old man knew what he was about.

The sun shone hotly down and not a cloud was to be seen in the sky. The road was very dusty, for many people who were all bound for the fair were driving, or riding, or walking upon it. There was no shelter anywhere from the sunbeams.

Among the rest, a man was trudging along and driving a cow to the fair. The cow was as beautiful a creature as any cow can be.

"She gives good milk, I'm sure," said the peasant. "That would be a very good exchange—the cow for the horse."

"Hallo, you there with the cow!" he said. "I tell you what: I fancy a horse costs more than a cow, but I don't care for that. A cow would be more useful to me. If you like, we'll exchange."

"To be sure I will," said the man, and they exchanged accordingly.

So that was settled, and the peasant might have turned back, for he had done the business he came to do. But as he had once made up his mind to go to the fair, he determined to proceed, merely to have a look at it. And so he went on to the town with his cow.

Leading the animal, he strode sturdily on, and after a short time he overtook a man who was driving a sheep. It was a good fat sheep with a fine fleece on its back.

"I should like to have that fellow," said our peasant. "He would find plenty of grass by our palings, and in the winter we could keep him in the room with us. Perhaps it would be more practical to have a sheep instead of a cow. Shall we exchange?"

---

[6] **bartered**—exchanged.

The man with the sheep was quite ready and the bargain was struck. So our peasant went on in the highroad with his sheep.

Soon he overtook another man, who came into the road from a field, carrying a great goose under his arm.

"That's a heavy thing you have there. It has plenty of feathers and plenty of fat, and would look well tied to a string and paddling in the water at our place. That would be something for my old woman. She could make all kinds of profit out of it. How often she has said, 'If we only had a goose!' Now perhaps she can have one, and if possible it shall be hers. Shall we exchange? I'll give you my sheep for your goose and thank you into the bargain."

The other man had not the least objection. And accordingly they exchanged, and our peasant became the **proprietor**[7] of the goose.

By this time he was very near the town. The crowd on the highroad became greater and greater. There was quite a crush of men and cattle. They walked in the road, close by the palings, and at the barrier they even walked into the tollman's potato field, where his own fowl was strutting about with a string to its leg, lest it should take fright at the crowd and stray away, and so be lost. This fowl had short tail feathers, and winked with both its eyes, and looked very cunning. "Cluck, cluck!" said the fowl.

What it thought when it said this I cannot tell you, but directly our good man saw it, he thought, "That's the finest fowl I've ever seen in my life! Why, it's finer than our parson's brood hen. On my word, I should like to have that fowl. A fowl can always find a grain or two, and can almost keep itself. I think it would be a good exchange if I could get that for my goose."

"Shall we exchange?" he asked the toll taker.

"Exchange?" repeated the man. "Well, that would not be a bad thing."

---

[7] **proprietor**—owner.

And so they exchanged. The toll taker at the barrier kept the goose, and the peasant carried away the fowl.

Now he had done a good deal of business on his way to the fair, and he was hot and tired. He wanted something to eat and a glass of brandy to drink, and soon he was in front of the inn. He was just about to step in when the hostler[8] came out, so they met at the door. The hostler was carrying a sack.

"What have you in that sack?" asked the peasant.

"Rotten apples," answered the hostler. "A whole sackful of them—enough to feed the pigs with."

"Why, that's a terrible waste! I should like to take them to my old woman at home. Last year the old tree by the turf-hole bore only a single apple, and we kept it in the cupboard till it was quite rotten and spoiled. 'It was always property,' my old woman said. But here she could see a quantity of property—a whole sackful. Yes, I shall be glad to show them to her."

"What will you give me for the sackful?" asked the hostler.

"What will I give? I will give my fowl in exchange."

And he gave the fowl accordingly and received the apples, which he carried into the guest room. He leaned the sack carefully by the stove, and then went to the table. But the stove was hot: he had not thought of that. Many guests were present—horse dealers, oxherds, and two Englishmen. And the two Englishmen were so rich that their pockets bulged out with gold coins and almost burst. And they could bet too, as you shall hear. Hiss-s-s! hiss-s-s! What was that by the stove? The apples were beginning to roast!

"What is that?"

"Why, do you know—" said our peasant.

And he told the whole story of the horse he had changed for a cow, and all the rest of it, down to the apples.

---

[8] hostler—owner of the inn.

"Well, your old woman will give it to you well when you get home!" said one of the two Englishmen. "There will be a disturbance."

"What? Give me what?" said the peasant. "She will kiss me and say, 'What the old man does is always right.'"

"Shall we wager?" said the Englishman. "We'll wager coined gold by the ton—a hundred pounds to the hundredweight!"[9]

"A bushel will be enough," replied the peasant. "I can only set the bushel of apples against it, and I'll throw myself and my old woman into the bargain. And I fancy that's piling up the measure."

"Done! Taken!"

And the bet was made. The host's carriage came up, and the Englishmen got in and the peasant got in. Away they went, and soon they stopped before the peasant's farm.

"Good evening, old woman."

"Good evening, old man."

"I've made the exchange."

"Yes, you understand what you're about," said the woman. And she embraced him, and paid no attention to the strange guests, nor did she notice the sack.

"I got a cow in exchange for the horse," said he.

"Heaven be thanked!" said she. "What glorious milk we shall now have, and butter and cheese on the table. That was a most capital exchange!"

"Yes, but I changed the cow for a sheep."

"Ah, that's better still!" cried the wife. "You always think of everything. We have just pasture enough for a sheep. Ewe's[10] milk and cheese, and woolen jackets and stockings! The cow cannot give those, and her hairs will only come off. How you think of everything!"

"But I changed away the sheep for a goose."

---

[9] hundredweight—unit of weight equal to 100 pounds.

[10] Ewe's—from a female sheep.

"Then this year we shall really have roast goose to eat, my dear old man. You are always thinking of something to give me pleasure. How charming that is! We can let the goose walk about with a string to her leg, and she'll grow fatter still before we roast her."

"But I gave away the goose for a fowl," said the man.

"A fowl? That *was* a good exchange!" replied the woman. "The fowl will lay eggs and hatch them, and we shall have chickens. We shall have a whole poultry yard! Oh, that's just what I was wishing for."

"Yes, but I exchanged the fowl for a sack of shriveled apples."

"What! I must positively kiss you for that!" exclaimed the wife. "My dear good husband! Now I'll tell you something. Do you know, you had hardly left me this morning before I began thinking how I could give you something very nice this evening. I thought it should be pancakes with **savory**[11] herbs. I had eggs, and bacon too. But I lacked herbs. So I went over to the schoolmaster's, as they have herbs there, I know. But the schoolmistress is a mean woman, though she looks so sweet. I begged her to lend me a handful of herbs. 'Lend!' she answered me. 'Nothing at all grows in our garden, not even a shriveled apple. I could not even lend you a shriveled apple, my dear woman.' But now I can lend *her* ten, or a whole sackful. That I'm very glad of. That makes me laugh." And with that she gave him a sounding kiss.

"I like that!" exclaimed both the Englishmen together. "Always going downhill, and always merry! That's worth the money."

So they paid a hundredweight of gold to the peasant, who was not scolded, but kissed.

Yes, it always pays, when the wife sees and always asserts that her husband knows best and that whatever he does is right.

---

[11] **savory**—appetizing; tasty; pleasantly pungent, spicy, not sweet.

You see, that is my story. I heard it when I was a child. And now you have heard it too, and know that "What the good man does is always right."

QUESTIONS TO CONSIDER

1. How does this story reinforce gender stereotypes? List all the stereotypes of both women and men that you find in this story. After each one, explain why it constitutes a stereotype.

2. What is the moral of this story? How might the moral of the story change if it were revised today?

3. In the end, which character do you think proves to be the smartest overall, and why? Who do you think ends up being the fool?

4. What cultural influences, including fairy tales, do you think prompt young children to develop sexist attitudes? In general, who do you think is limited more by such views—girls or boys? Why?

Why I Live at the P.O.

BY EUDORA WELTY

*A skilled and imaginative storyteller, Eudora Welty (1909–)
captures the language, lifestyle, wit, and energy of poor and working
class people in the South. Welty began writing short stories when
she was in her early twenties. In 1972 she won a Pulitzer Prize for
her novel,* The Optimist's Daughter. *The following story is about
a girl who leaves home to go live at the post office (the P.O.). The
story so inspired Steve Dorner, creator of a popular Internet e-mail
software program, that he named the program Eudora.*

I was getting along fine with Mama, Papa-Daddy
and Uncle Rondo until my sister Stella-Rondo just sepa-
rated from her husband and came back home again. Mr.
Whitaker! Of course I went with Mr. Whitaker first,
when he first appeared here in China Grove, taking
"Pose Yourself" photos, and Stella-Rondo broke us up.
Told him I was one-sided. Bigger on one side than the

other, which is a deliberate, **calculated**[1] falsehood: I'm the same. Stella-Rondo is exactly twelve months to the day younger than I am and for that reason she's spoiled.

She's always had anything in the world she wanted and then she'd throw it away. Papa-Daddy gave her this gorgeous Add-a-Pearl necklace[2] when she was eight years old and she threw it away playing baseball when she was nine, with only two pearls.

So as soon as she got married and moved away from home the first thing she did was separate! From Mr. Whitaker! This photographer with the popeyes she said she trusted. Came home from one of those towns up in Illinois and to our complete surprise brought this child of two.

Mama said she like to made her drop dead for a second. "Here you had this marvelous blonde child and never so much as wrote your mother a word about it," says Mama. "I'm thoroughly ashamed of you." But of course she wasn't.

Stella-Rondo just calmly takes off this *hat*, I wish you could see it. She says, "Why, Mama, Shirley-T.'s adopted. I can prove it."

"How?" says Mama, but all I says was, "H'm!" There I was over the hot stove, trying to stretch two chickens over five people and a completely unexpected child into the bargain, without one moment's notice.

"What do you mean—'H'm!'?" says Stella-Rondo, and Mama says, "I heard that, Sister."

I said that oh, I didn't mean a thing, only that whoever Shirley-T. was, she was the spit-image[3] of Papa-Daddy if he'd cut off his beard, which of course he'd never do in the world. Papa-Daddy's Mama's papa and sulks.

---

[1] **calculated**—planned; intended.

[2] An Add-a-Pearl necklace was an affordable way to purchase a genuine pearl necklace. Each year, one pearl was purchased and added to the chain.

[3] spit-image—looks exactly like. Sister is saying that the child looks like one of the family.

Stella-Rondo got furious! She said, "Sister, I don't need to tell you you got a lot of nerve and always did have and I'll thank you to make no future reference to my adopted child whatsoever."

"Very well," I said. "Very well, very well. Of course I noticed at once she looks like Mr. Whitaker's side too. That frown. She looks like a cross between Mr. Whitaker and Papa-Daddy."

"Well, all I can say is she isn't."

"She looks exactly like Shirley Temple to me," says Mama, but Shirley-T. just ran away from her.

So the first thing Stella-Rondo did at the table was turn Papa-Daddy against me.

"Papa-Daddy," she says. He was trying to cut up his meat. "Papa-Daddy!" I was taken completely by surprise. Papa-Daddy is about a million years old and's got this long-long beard. "Papa-Daddy, Sister says she fails to understand why you don't cut off your beard."

So Papa-Daddy l-a-y-s down his knife and fork! He's real rich. Mama says he is, he says he isn't. So he says, "Have I heard correctly? You don't understand why I don't cut off my beard?"

"Why," I says, "Papa-Daddy, of course I understand, I did not say any such of a thing, the idea!"

He says, "Hussy!"[4]

I says, "Papa-Daddy, you know I wouldn't any more want you to cut off your beard than the man in the moon. It was the farthest thing from my mind! Stella-Rondo sat there and made that up while she was eating breast of chicken."

But he says, "So the postmistress fails to understand why I don't cut off my beard. Which job I got you through my influence with the government. 'Bird's nest'—is that what you call it?"

---

[4] Hussy—a derogatory term meaning a bold, disrespectful, or mischievous girl. Papa-Daddy uses this term because he feels she is disrespectful in questioning his beard.

Not that it isn't the next to smallest P.O. in the entire state of Mississippi.

I says, "Oh, Papa-Daddy," I says, "I didn't say any such of a thing, I never dreamed it was a bird's nest, I have always been grateful though this is the next to smallest P.O. in the state of Mississippi, and I do not enjoy being referred to as a hussy by my own grandfather."

But Stella-Rondo says, "Yes, you did say it too. Anybody in the world could of heard you, that had ears."

"Stop right there," says Mama, looking at *me*.

So I pulled my napkin straight back through the napkin ring and left the table.

As soon as I was out of the room Mama says, "Call her back, or she'll starve to death," but Papa-Daddy says, "This is the beard I started growing on the Coast when I was fifteen years old." He would of gone on till nightfall if Shirley-T. hadn't lost the Milky Way she ate in Cairo.

So Papa-Daddy says, "I am going out and lie in the hammock, and you can all sit here and remember my words: I'll never cut off my beard as long as I live, even one inch, and I don't appreciate it in you at all." Passed right by me in the hall and went straight out and got in the hammock.

It would be a holiday. It wasn't five minutes before Uncle Rondo suddenly appeared in the hall in one of Stella-Rondo's flesh-colored kimonos,[5] all cut on the bias, like something Mr. Whitaker probably thought was gorgeous.

"Uncle Rondo!" I says. "I didn't know who that was! Where are you going?"

"Sister," he says, "get out of my way, I'm poisoned."

"If you're poisoned stay away from Papa-Daddy," I says. "Keep out of the hammock. Papa-Daddy will

---

[5] kimonos—loose dressing gowns tied with a sash, in imitation of a traditional Japanese outer garment. "Cut on the bias" refers to the way the material is cut across the grain of the fabric to make it drape attractively. Uncle Rondo is wearing a woman's robe.

certainly beat you on the head if you come within forty miles of him. He thinks I deliberately said he ought to cut off his beard after he got me the P.O., and I've told him and told him and told him, and he acts like he just don't hear me. Papa-Daddy must of gone stone deaf."

"He picked a fine day to do it then," says Uncle Rondo, and before you could say "Jack Robinson" flew out in the yard.

What he'd really done, he'd drunk another bottle of that prescription. He does it every single Fourth of July as sure as shooting, and it's horribly expensive. Then he falls over in the hammock and snores. So he insisted on zigzagging right on out to the hammock, looking like a half-wit.

Papa-Daddy woke up with this horrible yell and right there without moving an inch he tried to turn Uncle Rondo against me. I heard every word he said. Oh, he told Uncle Rondo I didn't learn to read till I was eight years old and he didn't see how in the world I ever got the mail put up at the P.O., much less read it all, and he said if Uncle Rondo could only fathom the lengths he had gone to get me that job! And he said on the other hand he thought Stella-Rondo had a brilliant mind and deserved credit for getting out of town. All the time he was just lying there swinging as pretty as you please and looping out his beard, and poor Uncle Rondo was *pleading* with him to slow down the hammock, it was making him as dizzy as a witch to watch it. But that's what Papa-Daddy likes about a hammock. So Uncle Rondo was too dizzy to get turned against me for the time being. He's Mama's only brother and is a good case of a one-track mind. Ask anybody. A certified pharmacist.

Just then I heard Stella-Rondo raising the upstairs window. While she was married she got this peculiar idea that it's cooler with the windows shut and locked. So she has to raise the window before she can make a soul hear her outdoors.

So she raises the window and says, "*Oh!*" You would have thought she was mortally wounded.

Uncle Rondo and Papa-Daddy didn't even look up, but kept right on with what they were doing. I had to laugh.

I flew up the stairs and threw the door open! I says, "What in the wide world's the matter, Stella-Rondo? You mortally wounded?"

"No," she says, "I am not mortally wounded but I wish you would do me the favor of looking out that window there and telling me what you see."

So I shade my eyes and look out the window.

"I see the front yard," I says.

"Don't you see any human beings?" she says.

"I see Uncle Rondo trying to run Papa-Daddy out of the hammock," I says. "Nothing more. Naturally, it's so suffocating-hot in the house, with all the windows shut and locked, everybody who cares to stay in their right mind will have to go out and get in the hammock before the Fourth of July is over."

"Don't you notice anything different about Uncle Rondo?" asks Stella-Rondo.

"Why, no, except he's got on some terrible-looking flesh-colored **contraption**[6] I wouldn't be found dead in, is all I can see," I says.

"Never mind, you won't be found dead in it, because it happens to be part of my trousseau,[7] and Mr. Whitaker took several dozen photographs of me in it," says Stella-Rondo. "What on earth could Uncle Rondo *mean* by wearing part of my trousseau out in the broad open daylight without saying so much as 'Kiss my foot,' *knowing* I only got home this morning after my

---

[6] **contraption**—mechanical device. Sister is using a word not usually associated with a dressing gown in order to insult Stella-Rondo.

[7] trousseau—clothing brought by a bride to her new home. A trousseau usually consists of lacy nightgowns, underwear, and so forth.

separation and hung my negligee[8] up on the bathroom door, just as nervous as I could be?"

"I'm sure I don't know, and what do you expect me to do about it?" I says. "Jump out the window?"

"No, I expect nothing of the kind. I simply declare that Uncle Rondo looks like a fool in it, that's all," she says. "It makes me sick to my stomach."

"Well, he looks as good as he can," I says. "As good as anybody in reason could." I stood up for Uncle Rondo, please remember. And I said to Stella-Rondo, "I think I would do well not to criticize so freely if I were you and came home with a two-year-old child I had never said a word about, and no explanation whatever about my separation."

"I asked you the instant I entered this house not to refer one more time to my adopted child, and you gave me your word of honor you would not," was all Stella-Rondo would say, and started pulling out every one of her eyebrows with some cheap Kress tweezers.

So I merely slammed the door behind me and went down and made some green-tomato pickle. Somebody had to do it. Of course Mama had turned both the Negroes loose; she always said no earthly power could hold one anyway on the Fourth of July, so she wouldn't even try. It turned out that Jaypan fell in the lake and came within a very narrow limit of drowning.

So Mama trots in. Lifts up the lid and says, "H'm! Not very good for your Uncle Rondo in his **precarious**[9] condition, I must say. Or poor little adopted Shirley-T. Shame on you!"

That made me tired. I says, "Well, Stella-Rondo had better thank her lucky stars it was her instead of me came trotting in with that very peculiar-looking child.

---

[8] negligee—woman's loose, flowing nightgown or robe. This is a French word. By having her use this word, the author is letting us know Stella-Rondo puts on airs.

[9] **precarious**—uncertain; hazardous.

Now if it had been me that trotted in from Illinois and brought a peculiar-looking child of two, I shudder to think of the reception I'd of got, much less controlled the diet of an entire family."

"But you must remember, Sister, that you were never married to Mr. Whitaker in the first place and didn't go up to Illinois to live," says Mama, shaking a spoon in my face. "If you had I would of been just as overjoyed to see you and your little adopted girl as I was to see Stella-Rondo, when you wound up with your separation and came on back home."

"You would not," I says.

"Don't contradict me, I would," says Mama.

But I said she couldn't convince me though she talked till she was blue in the face. Then I said, "Besides, you know as well as I do that that child is not adopted."

"She most certainly is adopted," says Mama, stiff as a poker.

I says, "Why, Mama, Stella-Rondo had her just as sure as anything in this world, and just too stuck up to admit it."

"Why, Sister," said Mama. "Here I thought we were going to have a pleasant Fourth of July, and you start right out not believing a word your own baby sister tells you!"

"Just like Cousin Annie Flo. Went to her grave denying the facts of life," I remind Mama.

"I told you if you ever mentioned Annie Flo's name I'd slap your face," says Mama, and slaps my face.

"All right, you wait and see," I says.

"I," says Mama, "*I* prefer to take my children's word for anything when it's humanly possible." You ought to see Mama, she weighs two hundred pounds and has real tiny feet.

Just then something perfectly horrible occurred to me.

"Mama," I says, "can that child talk?" I simply had to whisper! "Mama, I wonder if that child can be—you know—in any way? Do you realize," I says, "that she hasn't spoken one single, solitary word to a human being up to this minute? This is the way she looks," I says, and I looked like this.

Well, Mama and I just stood there and stared at each other. It was horrible!

"I remember well that Joe Whitaker frequently drank like a fish," says Mama. "I believed to my soul he drank *chemicals*." And without another word she marches to the foot of the stairs and calls Stella-Rondo.

"Stella-Rondo? O-o-o-o-o! Stella-Rondo!"

"What?" says Stella-Rondo from upstairs. Not even the grace to get up off the bed.

"Can that child of yours talk?" asks Mama.

Stella-Rondo says, "Can she what?"

"Talk! Talk!" says Mama. "Burdyburdyburdyburdy!"

So Stella-Rondo yells back, "Who says she can't talk?"

"Sister says so," says Mama.

"You didn't have to tell me, I know whose word of honor don't mean a thing in this house," says Stella-Rondo.

And in a minute the loudest Yankee[10] voice I ever heard in my life yells out, "OE'm Pop-OE the Sailor-r-r-r Ma-a-an!" and then somebody jumps up and down in the upstairs hall. In another second the house would of fallen down.

"Not only talks, she can tap-dance!" calls Stella-Rondo. "Which is more than some people I won't name can do."

"Why, the little precious darling thing!" Mama says, so surprised. "Just as smart as she can be!" Starts talking baby talk right there. Then she turns on me. "Sister, you ought to be thoroughly ashamed! Run upstairs this instant and apologize to Stella-Rondo and Shirley-T."

"Apologize for what?" I says. "I merely wondered if the child was normal, that's all. Now that she's proved she is, why, I have nothing further to say."

---

[10] Yankee—Northern. Shirley-T has been living in Illinois since she was born and has an accent different from that of the family in Mississippi.

But Mama just turned on her heel and flew out, furious. She ran right upstairs and hugged the baby. She believed it was adopted. Stella-Rondo hadn't done a thing but turn her against me from upstairs while I stood there helpless over the hot stove. So that made Mama, Papa-Daddy and the baby all on Stella-Rondo's side.

Next, Uncle Rondo.

I must say that Uncle Rondo has been marvelous to me at various times in the past and I was completely unprepared to be made to jump out of my skin, the way it turned out. Once Stella-Rondo did something perfectly horrible to him—broke a chain letter[11] from Flanders Field—and he took the radio back he had given her and gave it to me. Stella-Rondo was furious! For six months we all had to call her Stella instead of Stella-Rondo, or she wouldn't answer. I always thought Uncle Rondo had all the brains of the entire family. Another time he sent me to Mammoth Cave, with all expenses paid.

But this would be the day he was drinking that prescription, the Fourth of July.

So at supper Stella-Rondo speaks up and says she thinks Uncle Rondo ought to try to eat a little something. So finally Uncle Rondo said he would try a little cold biscuits and ketchup, but that was all. So *she* brought it to him.

"Do you think it wise to disport[12] with ketchup in Stella-Rondo's flesh-colored kimono?" I says. Trying to be considerate! If Stella-Rondo couldn't watch out for her trousseau, somebody had to.

"Any objections?" asks Uncle Rondo, just about to pour out all the ketchup.

---

[11] chain letter—letter sent to a number of people, asking each to send a copy on to a number of others. Chain letters promise good things to those who keep the chain going and bad luck to those who don't. Sister would think it a patriotic duty to send on a letter from Flanders Field, where American soldiers are fighting the Germans in World War I.

[12] disport—amuse oneself.

"Don't mind what she says, Uncle Rondo," says Stella-Rondo. "Sister has been devoting this solid afternoon to sneering out my bedroom window at the way you look."

"What's that?" says Uncle Rondo. Uncle Rondo has got the most terrible temper in the world. Anything is liable to make him tear the house down if it comes at the wrong time.

So Stella-Rondo says, "Sister says, 'Uncle Rondo certainly does look like a fool in that pink kimono!'"

Do you remember who it was really said that?

Uncle Rondo spills out all the ketchup and jumps out of his chair and tears off the kimono and throws it down on the dirty floor and puts his foot on it. It had to be sent all the way to Jackson to the cleaners and re-pleated.

"So that's your opinion of your Uncle Rondo, is it?" he says. "I look like a fool, do I? Well, that's the last straw. A whole day in this house with nothing to do, and then to hear you come out with a remark like that behind my back!"

"I didn't say any such of a thing, Uncle Rondo," I says, "and I'm not saying who did, either. Why, I think you look all right. Just try to take care of yourself and not talk and eat at the same time," I says. "I think you better go lie down."

"Lie down my foot," says Uncle Rondo. I ought to of known by that he was fixing to do something perfectly horrible.

So he didn't do anything that night in the precarious state he was in—just played Casino with Mama and Stella-Rondo and Shirley-T. and gave Shirley-T. a nickel with a head on both sides. It tickled her nearly to death, and she called him "Papa." But at 6:30 A.M. the next morning, he threw a whole five-cent package of some unsold one-inch firecrackers from the store as hard as he could into my bedroom and they every one went off. Not one bad one in the string. Anybody else, there'd be one that wouldn't go off.

Well, I'm just terribly susceptible to noise of any kind, the doctor has always told me I was the most sensitive person he had ever seen in his whole life, and I was simply **prostrated**.[13] I couldn't eat! People tell me they heard it as far as the cemetery, and old Aunt Jep Patterson, that had been holding her own so good, thought it was Judgment Day[14] and she was going to meet her whole family. It's usually so quiet here.

And I'll tell you it didn't take me any longer than a minute to make up my mind what to do. There I was with the whole entire house on Stella-Rondo's side and turned against me. If I have anything at all I have pride.

So I just decided I'd go straight down to the P.O. There's plenty of room there in the back, I says to myself.

Well! I made no bones about letting the family catch on to what I was up to. I didn't try to conceal it.

The first thing they knew, I marched in where they were all playing Old Maid and pulled the electric **oscillating**[15] fan out by the plug, and everything got real hot. Next I snatched the pillow I'd done the needlepoint on right off the davenport[16] from behind Papa-Daddy. He went "Ugh!" I beat Stella-Rondo up the stairs and finally found my charm bracelet in her bureau drawer under a picture of Nelson Eddy.[17]

"So that's the way the land lies," says Uncle Rondo. There he was, piecing on[18] the ham. "Well, Sister, I'll be glad to donate my army cot if you got any place to set it up, providing you'll leave right this minute and let me get some peace." Uncle Rondo was in France.[19]

---

[13] **prostrated**—laid out face down on the ground.

[14] Judgment Day—in some religions, the day that God judges all people. It is considered the final judgment at the end of the world. The loud noise convinced Aunt Jep that the time had come.

[15] **oscillating**—moving back and forth.

[16] davenport—sofa.

[17] Nelson Eddy—a popular singer in the 1930s.

[18] piecing on—picking at, nibbling on.

[19] This is a reference to the fact that he had fought in World War I.

"Thank you kindly for the cot and 'peace' is hardly the word I would select if I had to resort to firecrackers at 6:30 A.M. in a young girl's bedroom," I says back to him. "And as to where I intend to go, you seem to forget my position as postmistress of China Grove, Mississippi," I says. "I've always got the P.O."

Well, that made them all sit up and take notice.

I went out front and started digging up some four-o'clocks[20] to plant around the P.O.

"Ah-ah-ah!" says Mama, raising the window. "Those happen to be my four-o'clocks. Everything planted in that star is mine. I've never known you to make anything grow in your life."

"Very well," I says. "But I take the fern. Even you, Mama, can't stand there and deny that I'm the one watered that fern. And I happen to know where I can send in a box top and get a packet of one thousand mixed seeds, no two the same kind, free."

"Oh, where?" Mama wants to know.

But I says, "Too late. You 'tend to your house, and I'll 'tend to mine. You hear things like that all the time if you know how to listen to the radio. Perfectly marvelous offers. Get anything you want free."

So I hope to tell you I marched in and got that radio, and they could of all bit a nail in two, especially Stella-Rondo, that it used to belong to, and she well knew she couldn't get it back, I'd sue for it like a shot. And I very politely took the sewing-machine motor I helped pay the most on to give Mama for Christmas back in 1929, and a good big calendar, with the first-aid remedies on it. The thermometer and the Hawaiian ukulele[21] certainly were rightfully mine, and I stood on the stepladder and got all my watermelon-rind preserves and every fruit and vegetable I'd put up, every jar. Then I began to pull the

---

[20] four-o'clocks—fragrant flowers that open in the late afternoon and close the next morning.

[21] ukulele—small, four-stringed guitar.

tacks out of the bluebird wall vases on the archway to the dining room.

"Who told you you could have those, Miss Priss?" says Mama, fanning as hard as she could.

"I bought 'em and I'll keep track of 'em," I says. "I'll tack 'em up one on each side the post-office window, and you can see 'em when you come to ask me for your mail, if you're so dead to see 'em."

"Not I! I'll never darken the door to that post office again if I live to be a hundred," Mama says. "Ungrateful child! After all the money we spent on you at the Normal."[22]

"Me either," says Stella-Rondo. "You can just let my mail lie there and rot, for all I care. I'll never come and relieve you of a single, solitary piece."

"I should worry," I says. "And who you think's going to sit down and write you all those big fat letters and post-cards, by the way? Mr. Whitaker? Just because he was the only man ever dropped down in China Grove and you got him—unfairly—is he going to sit down and write you a lengthy correspondence after you come home giving no rhyme nor reason whatsoever for your separation and no explanation for the presence of that child? I may not have your brilliant mind, but I fail to see it."

So Mama says, "Sister, I've told you a thousand times that Stella-Rondo simply got homesick, and this child is far too big to be hers," and she says, "Now, why don't you all just sit down and play Casino?"

Then Shirley-T. sticks out her tongue at me in this perfectly horrible way. She has no more manners than the man in the moon. I told her she was going to cross her eyes like that some day and they'd stick.

"It's too late to stop me now," I says. "You should have tried that yesterday. I'm going to the P.O. and the only way you can possibly see me is to visit me there."

---

[22] Normal—teacher-training college.

So Papa-Daddy says, "You'll never catch me setting foot in that post office, even if I should take a notion into my head to write a letter some place." He says, "I won't have you reachin' out of that little old window with a pair of shears and cuttin' off any beard of mine. I'm too smart for you!"

"We all are," says Stella-Rondo.

But I said, "If you're so smart, where's Mr. Whitaker?"

So then Uncle Rondo says, "I'll thank you from now on to stop reading all the orders I get on postcards and telling everybody in China Grove what you think is the matter with them," but I says, "I draw my own conclusions and will continue in the future to draw them." I says, "If people want to write their inmost secrets on penny postcards, there's nothing in the wide world you can do about it, Uncle Rondo."

"And if you think we'll ever *write* another postcard you're sadly mistaken," says Mama.

"Cutting off your nose to spite your face then," I says. "But if you're all determined to have no more to do with the U.S. mail, think of this: What will Stella-Rondo do now, if she wants to tell Mr. Whitaker to come after her?"

"Wah!" says Stella-Rondo. I knew she'd cry. She had a conniption fit[23] right there in the kitchen.

"It will be interesting to see how long she holds out," I says. "And now—I am leaving."

"Good-bye," says Uncle Rondo.

"Oh, I declare," says Mama, "to think that a family of mine should quarrel on the Fourth of July, or the day after, over Stella-Rondo leaving old Mr. Whitaker and having the sweetest little adopted child! It looks like we'd all be glad!"

"Wah!" says Stella-Rondo, and has a fresh conniption fit.

---

[23] conniption fit—fit of anger or hysterics.

"He left *her*—you mark my words," I says. "That's Mr. Whitaker. I know Mr. Whitaker. After all, I knew him first. I said from the beginning he'd up and leave her. I foretold every single thing that's happened."

"Where did he go?" asks Mama.

"Probably to the North Pole, if he knows what's good for him," I says.

But Stella-Rondo just bawled and wouldn't say another word. She flew to her room and slammed the door.

"Now look what you've gone and done, Sister," says Mama. "You go apologize."

"I haven't got time, I'm leaving," I says.

"Well, what are you waiting around for?" asks Uncle Rondo.

So I just picked up the kitchen clock and marched off, without saying "Kiss my foot" or anything, and never did tell Stella-Rondo good-bye.

There was a girl going along on a little wagon right in front.

"Girl," I says, "come help me haul these things down the hill, I'm going to live in the post office."

Took her nine trips in her express wagon. Uncle Rondo came out on the porch and threw her a nickel.

And that's the last I've laid eyes on any of my family or my family laid eyes on me for five solid days and nights. Stella-Rondo may be telling the most horrible tales in the world about Mr. Whitaker, but I haven't heard them. As I tell everybody, I draw my own conclusions.

But oh, I like it here. It's ideal, as I've been saying. You see, I've got everything cater-cornered,[24] the way I like it. Hear the radio? All the war news. Radio, sewing machine, book ends, ironing board and that great big piano lamp—peace, that's what I like. Butter-bean vines planted all along the front where the strings are.

---

[24] cater-cornered—set diagonally.

Of course, there's not much mail. My family are naturally the main people in China Grove, and if they prefer to vanish from the face of the earth, for all the mail they get or the mail they write, why, I'm not going to open my mouth. Some of the folks here in town are taking up for me and some turned against me. I know which is which. There are always people who will quit buying stamps just to get on the right side of Papa-Daddy.

But here I am, and here I'll stay. I want the world to know I'm happy.

And if Stella-Rondo should come to me this minute, on bended knees, and *attempt* to explain the incidents of her life with Mr. Whitaker, I'd simply put my fingers in both my ears and refuse to listen.

QUESTIONS TO CONSIDER

1. What happened in the past that might explain the tension between Stella-Rondo and Sister?

2. What does Stella-Rondo's story suggest about the role of women in the years following World War I?

3. What does Sister's name tell you about how she is seen within her family? How might her name influence how she sees herself?

4. What do you think the P.O. represents to Sister as she begins the process of separating from her family?

5. What family items and values does Sister take when she leaves home? Why? What other parts of her family history and values do you think she took with her, even if she did not choose them?

6. In what ways is Sister a rebel?

When I Was Growing Up

BY NELLIE WONG

Nellie Wong, a Chinese-American writer, uses themes of race and gender throughout her work. Her collections of poetry include Death of Long Stream Lady *and* Stolen Moments *(1997), in which the following poem appears. In this poem Wong uses powerful images and descriptions to communicate her feelings and experiences as a Chinese girl growing up in America and wanting so much to "fit in."*

I know now that once I longed to be white.
How? you ask.
Let me tell you the ways.

when I was growing up, people told me
I was dark and I believed my own darkness
in the mirror, in my soul, my own narrow vision

when I was growing up, my sisters
with fair skin got praised
for their beauty, and in the dark
I fell further, crushed between high walls

when I was growing up, I read magazines
and saw movies, blonde movie stars, white skin,
sensuous lips and to be elevated, to become
a woman, a desirable woman, I began to wear
imaginary pale skin

when I was growing up, I was proud
of my English, my grammar, my spelling
fitting into the group of smart children
smart Chinese children, fitting in,
belonging, getting in line

when I was growing up and went to high school,
I discovered the rich white girls, a few yellow girls,
their imported cotton dresses, their cashmere sweaters,
their curly hair and I thought that I too should have
what these lucky girls had

when I was growing up, I hungered
for American food, American styles,
coded: white and even to me, a child
born of Chinese parents, being Chinese
was feeling foreign, was limiting,
was unAmerican

when I was growing up and a white man wanted
to take me out, I thought I was special,
an exotic gardenia, anxious to fit
the stereotype of an oriental chick

when I was growing up, I felt ashamed
of some yellow men, their small bones,
their frail bodies, their spitting
on the streets, their coughing,
their lying in sunless rooms,
shooting themselves in the arms

when I was growing up, people would ask
if I were Filipino, Polynesian, Portuguese.
They named all colors except white, the shell
of my soul, but not my dark, rough skin

when I was growing up, I felt
dirty. I thought that god
made white people clean
and no matter how much I bathed,
I could not change, I could not shed
my skin in the gray water

when I was growing up, I swore
I would run away to purple mountains,
houses by the sea with nothing over
my head, with space to breathe,
uncongested with yellow people in an area
called Chinatown, in an area I later learned
was a ghetto, one of many hearts
of Asian America

I know now that once I longed to be white
How many more ways? you ask.
Haven't I told you enough?

QUESTIONS TO CONSIDER

1. What was it like for Nellie Wong to grow up Chinese in America?

2. Why did Wong compare herself to white girls? What did being white seem to represent?

3. What do you think happens when you try to be something or be like someone that you are not? What do you think happened to Wong?

4. Why do you think Wong wrote this poem? How do you think she feels now about herself and about her longing to be white as a girl?

Ruth's Song (Because She Could Not Sing It)

BY GLORIA STEINEM

Gloria Steinem (1934–   ) is a strong feminist, political activist, and advocate of the women's movement. After graduating from Smith College in 1956 she wrote for television and magazines. Steinem became active in the women's liberation movement in the late sixties. She worked for the rights of women in the workplace and helped encourage women to run for political office through the establishment of the National Women's Political Caucus in 1971. The next year she founded Ms., *a magazine published by and written for women. Her books include:* Revolution from Within *and* Moving Beyond Words. *The following essay is taken from a collection of articles titled* Outrageous Acts and Everyday Rebellions *(1983). In "Ruth's Song," Steinem examines her own childhood with her mother, Ruth, as she explores societal and gender issues.*

Happy or unhappy, families are all mysterious. We have only to imagine how differently we would be described—and will be, after our deaths—by each of the family members who believe they know us. The only question is, Why are some mysteries more important than others?

The fate of my Uncle Ed was a mystery of importance in our family. We lavished years of speculation on his transformation from a brilliant young electrical engineer to the town handyman. What could have changed this elegant, Lincolnesque[1] student voted "Best Dressed" by his classmates to the **gaunt**,[2] unshaven man I remember? Why did he leave a young son and a first wife of the "proper" class and religion, marry a much less educated woman of the "wrong" religion, and raise a second family in a house near an abandoned airstrip; a house whose walls were patched with metal signs to stop the wind? Why did he never talk about his transformation?

For years, I assumed that some secret and dramatic events of a year he spent in Alaska had made the difference. Then I discovered that the trip had come after his change and probably been made because of it. Strangers he worked for as a much-loved handyman talked about him as one more tragedy of the Depression, and it was true that Uncle Ed's father, my paternal grandfather, had lost his money in the stockmarket Crash and died of (depending on who was telling the story) pneumonia or a broken heart. But the Crash of 1929 also had come long after Uncle Ed's transformation. Another theory was that he was afflicted with a mental problem that lasted most of his life, yet he was supremely competent at his work, led an independent life, and asked for help from no one.

Perhaps he had fallen under the spell of a radical professor in the early days of the century, the height of this country's romance with socialism and anarchism.[3]

---

[1] Lincolnesque—resembling Abraham Lincoln's build—tall, thin, angular.

[2] **gaunt**—extremely thin.

[3] socialism and anarchism—Socialism is a political philosophy that believes workers should have political power so that material goods and political influence are evenly distributed throughout all classes of a society. Anarchism is a political philosophy that teaches that all forms of political power are oppressive and should be eliminated.

That was the theory of another uncle on my mother's side. I do remember that no matter how much Uncle Ed needed money, he would charge no more for his work than materials plus 10 percent, and I never saw him in anything other than ancient boots and overalls held up with strategic safety pins. Was he really trying to replace socialism-in-one-country with socialism-in-one-man? If so, why did my grandmother, a woman who herself had run for the school board in coalition with anarchists and socialists, mistrust his judgment so much that she left his share of her estate in trust, even though he was over fifty when she died? And why did Uncle Ed seem uninterested in all other political words and acts? Was it true instead that, as another relative insisted, Uncle Ed had chosen poverty to disprove the myths of Jews and money?

Years after my uncle's death, I asked a son in his second family if he had the key to this family mystery. No, he said. He had never known his father any other way. For that cousin, there had been no question. For the rest of us, there was to be no answer.

For many years I also never imagined my mother any way other than the person she had become before I was born. She was just a fact of life when I was growing up; someone to be worried about and cared for; an **invalid**[4] who lay in bed with eyes closed and lips moving in occasional response to voices only she could hear; a woman to whom I brought an endless stream of toast and coffee, bologna sandwiches and dime pies, in a child's version of what meals should be. She was a loving, intelligent, terrorized woman who tried hard to clean our littered house whenever she emerged from her private world, but who could rarely be counted on to finish one task. In many ways, our roles were reversed: I was the mother and she was the child. Yet that didn't help her, for she still worried about me with all the

---

[4] **invalid**—sickly person.

intensity of a frightened mother, plus the special fears of her own world full of threats and hostile voices.

Even then I suppose I must have known that, years before she was thirty-five and I was born, she had been a spirited adventurous young woman who struggled out of a working-class family and into college, who found work she loved and continued to do, even after she was married and my older sister was there to be cared for. Certainly, our immediate family and nearby relatives, of whom I was by far the youngest, must have remembered her life as a whole and functioning person. She was thirty before she gave up her own career to help my father run the Michigan summer resort that was the most practical of his many dreams, and she worked hard there as everything from bookkeeper to bar manager. The family must have watched this energetic, fun-loving, book-loving woman turn into someone who was afraid to be alone, who could not hang on to reality long enough to hold a job, and who could rarely concentrate enough to read a book.

Yet I don't remember any family speculation about the mystery of my mother's transformation. To the kind ones and those who liked her, this new Ruth was simply a sad event, perhaps a mental case, a family problem to be accepted and cared for until some natural process made her better. To the less kind or those who had resented her earlier independence, she was a willful failure, someone who lived in a filthy house, a woman who simply would not pull herself together.

Unlike the case of my Uncle Ed, exterior events were never suggested as reason enough for her problems. Giving up her own career was never cited as her personal parallel of the Depression. (Nor was there discussion of the Depression itself, though my mother, like millions of others, had made potato soup and cut up blankets to make my sister's winter clothes.) Her fears of dependence and poverty were no match for my uncle's possible political beliefs. The real influence of newspaper editors who had praised her reporting was not taken as seriously as the possible influence of one radical professor.

Even the explanation of mental illness seemed to contain more personal fault when applied to my mother. She had suffered her first "nervous breakdown," as she and everyone else called it, before I was born and when my sister was about five. It followed years of trying to take care of a baby, be the wife of a kind but financially irresponsible man with showbusiness dreams, and still keep her much-loved job as reporter and newspaper editor. After many months in a sanatorium,[5] she was pronounced recovered. That is, she was able to take care of my sister again, to move away from the city and the job she loved, and to work with my father at the isolated rural lake in Michigan he was trying to transform into a resort worthy of the big dance bands of the 1930s.

But she was never again completely without the spells of depression, anxiety, and visions into some other world that eventually were to turn her into the non-person I remember. And she was never again without a bottle of dark, acrid-smelling[6] liquid she called "Doc Howard's medicine": a solution of chloral hydrate that I later learned was the main ingredient of "Mickey Finns" or "knockout drops," and that probably made my mother and her doctor the pioneers of modern tranquilizers. Though friends and relatives saw this medicine as one more evidence of weakness and indulgence, to me it always seemed an embarrassing but necessary evil. It slurred her speech and slowed her coordination, making our neighbors and my school friends believe she was a drunk. But without it, she would not sleep for days, even a week at a time, and her feverish eyes began to see only that private world in which wars and hostile voices threatened the people she loved.

---

[5] sanatorium—institution for the treatment of mental illness.

[6] acrid-smelling—sharp- or bitter-smelling.

Because my parents had divorced and my sister was working in a faraway city, my mother and I were alone together then, living off the **meager**[7] fixed income that my mother got from leasing her share of the remaining land in Michigan. I remember a long Thanksgiving weekend spent hanging on to her with one hand and holding my eighth-grade assignment of *Tale of Two Cities* in the other, because the war[8] outside our house was so real to my mother that she had plunged her hand through a window, badly cutting her arm in an effort to help us escape. Only when she finally agreed to swallow the medicine could she sleep, and only then could I end the terrible calm that comes with crisis and admit to myself how afraid I had been.

No wonder that no relative in my memory challenged the doctor who prescribed this medicine, asked if some of her suffering and hallucinating might be due to overdose or withdrawal, or even consulted another doctor about its use. It was our relief as well as hers.

But why was she never returned even to that first sanatorium? Or to help that might come from other doctors? It's hard to say. Partly, it was her own fear of returning. Partly, it was too little money, and a family's not-unusual assumption that mental illness is an inevitable part of someone's personality. Or perhaps other family members had feared something like my experience when, one hot and desperate summer between the sixth and seventh grade, I finally persuaded her to let me take her to the only doctor from those sanatorium days whom she remembered without fear.

Yes, this **brusque**[9] old man told me after talking to my abstracted, timid mother for twenty minutes: she definitely belongs in a state hospital. I should put her there right away. But even at that age, *Life* magazine and newspaper exposés had told me what horrors went on

---

[7] **meager**—scanty; small.

[8] the war—World War II.

[9] **brusque**—abrupt.

inside those hospitals. Assuming there to be no other alternative, I took her home and never tried again.

In retrospect, perhaps the biggest reason my mother was cared for but not helped for twenty years was the simplest: her functioning was not that necessary to the world. Like women alcoholics who drink in their kitchens while costly programs are constructed for executives who drink, or like the homemakers subdued with tranquilizers while male patients get therapy and personal attention instead, my mother was not an important worker. She was not even the caretaker of a very young child, as she had been when she was hospitalized the first time. My father had patiently brought home the groceries and kept our odd household going until I was eight or so and my sister went away to college. Two years later when wartime gas rationing closed his summer resort and he had to travel to buy and sell in summer as well as winter, he said: How can I travel and take care of your mother? How can I make a living? He was right. It was impossible to do both. I did not blame him for leaving once I was old enough to be the bringer of meals and answerer of my mother's questions. ("Has your sister been killed in a car crash?" "Are there German soldiers outside?") I replaced my father, my mother was left with one more way of maintaining a sad **status quo**,[10] and the world went on undisturbed.

That's why our lives, my mother's from forty-six to fifty-three, and my own from ten to seventeen, were spent alone together. There was one sane winter in a house we rented to be near my sister's college in Massachusetts, then one bad summer spent house-sitting in suburbia while my mother hallucinated and my sister struggled to hold down a summer job in New York. But the rest of those years were lived in Toledo where both my mother and father had been born, and on whose city newspapers an earlier Ruth had worked.

---

[10] **status quo**—existing condition or state of affairs.

First we moved into a basement apartment in a good neighborhood. In those rooms behind a furnace, I made one last stab at being a child. By pretending to be much sicker with a cold than I really was, I hoped my mother would suddenly turn into a sane and cheerful woman bringing me chicken soup à la Hollywood. Of course, she could not. It only made her feel worse that she could not. I stopped pretending.

But for most of those years, we lived in the upstairs of the house my mother had grown up in and her parents left her—a deteriorating farm house engulfed by the city, with poor but newer houses stacked against it and a major highway a few feet from its sagging front porch. For a while, we could rent the two downstairs apartments to a newlywed factory worker and a local butcher's family. Then the health department condemned our ancient furnace for the final time, sealing it so tight that even my resourceful Uncle Ed couldn't produce illegal heat.

In that house, I remember:

. . . lying in the bed my mother and I shared for warmth, listening on the early morning radio to the royal wedding of Princess Elizabeth and Prince Philip being broadcast live, while we tried to ignore and thus protect each other from the unmistakable sounds of the factory worker downstairs beating up and locking out his pregnant wife.

. . . hanging paper drapes I had bought in the dime store; stacking books and papers in the shape of two armchairs and covering them with blankets; evolving my own dishwashing system (I waited until all the dishes were dirty, then put them in the bathtub); and listening to my mother's high praise for these housekeeping efforts to bring order from chaos, though in retrospect I think they probably depressed her further.

. . . coming back from one of the Eagles' Club shows where I and other veterans of a local tap-dancing school made ten dollars a night for two shows, and finding my mother waiting with a flashlight and no coat in the dark cold of the bus stop, worried about my safety walking home.

. . . in a good period, when my mother's native adventurousness came through, answering a classified ad together for an amateur acting troupe that performed Biblical dramas in churches, and doing several very corny performances of *Noah's Ark* while my proud mother shook metal sheets backstage to make thunder.

. . . on a hot summer night, being bitten by one of the rats that shared our house and its back alley. It was a terrifying night that turned into a touching one when my mother, summoning courage from some unknown reservoir of love, became a calm, comforting parent who took me to a hospital emergency room despite her terror at leaving home.

. . . coming home from a local library with the three books a week into which I regularly escaped, and discovering that for once there was no need to escape. My mother was calmly planting hollyhocks[11] in the vacant lot next door.

But there were also times when she woke in the early winter dark, too frightened and disoriented to remember that I was at my usual after-school job, and so called the police to find me. Humiliated in front of my friends by sirens and policemen, I would yell at her—and she would bow her head in fear and say "I'm sorry, I'm sorry, I'm sorry," just as she had done so often when my otherwise-kindhearted father had yelled at her in frustration. Perhaps the worst thing about suffering is that it finally hardens the hearts of those around it.

And there were many, many times when I badgered her until her shaking hands had written a small check to cash at the corner grocery and I could leave her alone while I escaped to the comfort of well-heated dime

---

[11] hollyhocks—flowers with pink, red, yellow, or lavender blossoms that run up the stems.

stores that smelled of fresh doughnuts, or to air-conditioned Saturday-afternoon movies that were windows on a very different world.

But my ultimate protection was this: I was just passing through, a guest in the house; perhaps this wasn't my mother at all. Though I knew very well that I was her daughter, I sometimes imagined that I had been adopted and that my real parents would find me, a fantasy I've since discovered is common. (If children wrote more and grownups less, being adopted might be seen not only as a fear but also as a hope.) Certainly, I didn't mourn the wasted life of this woman who was scarcely older than I am now. I worried only about the times when she got worse.

Pity takes distance and a certainty of surviving. It was only after our house was bought for **demolition**[12] by the church next door, and after my sister had performed the miracle of persuading my father to give me a carefree time before college by taking my mother with him to California for a year, that I could afford to think about the sadness of her life. Suddenly, I was far away in Washington, living with my sister and sharing a house with several of her friends. While I finished high school and discovered to my surprise that my classmates felt sorry for me because my mother *wasn't* there, I also realized that my sister, at least in her early childhood, had known a very different person who lived inside our mother, an earlier Ruth.

She was a woman I met for the first time in a mental hospital near Baltimore, a **humane**[13] place with gardens and trees where I visited her each weekend of the summer after my first year away in college. Fortunately, my sister hadn't been able to work and be our mother's caretaker, too. After my father's year was up, my sister had carefully researched hospitals and found the courage to break the family chain.

---

[12] **demolition**—total destruction.

[13] **humane**—kind and compassionate.

At first, this Ruth was the same abstracted, frightened woman I had lived with all those years, though now all the sadder for being approached through long hospital corridors and many locked doors. But gradually she began to talk about her past life, memories that doctors there must have been awakening. I began to meet a Ruth I had never known.

. . . A tall, spirited, auburn-haired high-school girl who loved basketball and reading; who tried to drive her uncle's Stanley Steamer[14] when it was the first car in the neighborhood; who had a gift for gardening and who sometimes, in defiance of convention, wore her father's overalls; a girl with the courage to go to dances even though her church told her that music itself was sinful, and whose sense of adventure almost made up for feeling **gawky**[15] and unpretty next to her daintier, dark-haired sister.

. . . A very little girl, just learning to walk, discovering the body places where touching was pleasurable, and being punished by her mother who slapped her hard across the kitchen floor.

. . . A daughter of a handsome railroad-engineer and a schoolteacher who felt she had married "beneath her"; the mother who took her two daughters on Christmas trips to faraway New York on an engineer's free railroad pass and showed them the restaurants and theaters they should aspire to—even though they could only stand outside them in the snow.

. . . A good student at Oberlin College, whose free-thinking traditions she loved, where friends nicknamed her "Billy"; a student with a talent for both mathematics and poetry, who was not above putting an invisible film of Karo syrup on all the john seats in her dormitory the night of a big prom; a daughter who had to return to

---

[14] Stanley Steamer—American steam-driven automobile produced from 1897 until after World War I.

[15] **gawky**—clumsy, awkward.

Toledo, live with her family, and go to a local university when her ambitious mother—who had scrimped and saved, ghostwritten a minister's sermons, and made her daughters' clothes in order to get them to college at all—ran out of money. At home, this Ruth became a part-time bookkeeper in a lingerie shop for the very rich, commuting to classes and listening to her mother's harsh lectures on the security of becoming a teacher; but also a young woman who was still rebellious enough to fall in love with my father, the editor of her university newspaper, a funny and charming young man who was a terrible student, had no intention of graduating, put on all the campus dances, and was unacceptably Jewish.

I knew from family lore that my mother had married my father twice: once secretly, after he invited her to become the literary editor of his campus newspaper, and once a year later in a public ceremony, which some members of both families refused to attend as the "mixed marriage" of its day.

And I knew that my mother had gone on to earn a teaching certificate. She had used it to scare away truant officers during the winters when, after my father closed the summer resort for the season, we lived in a house trailer and worked our way to Florida or California and back by buying and selling antiques.

But only during those increasingly adventurous weekend outings from the hospital—going shopping, to lunch, to the movies—did I realize that she had taught college calculus for a year in deference to[16] her mother's insistence that she have teaching "to fall back on." And only then did I realize she had fallen in love with newspapers along with my father. After graduating from the university paper, she wrote a gossip column for a local **tabloid**,[17] under the name "Duncan MacKenzie," since women weren't supposed to do such things, and soon had earned a job as

---

[16] in deference to—out of respect for.

[17] **tabloid**—newspaper of small format giving news in condensed form, usually with sensational material.

society reporter on one of Toledo's two big dailies. By the time my sister was four or so, she had worked her way up to the coveted position of Sunday editor.

* * *

I know I will spend the next years figuring out what her life has left in me.

I realize that I've always been more touched by old people than by children. It's the talent and hopes locked up in a failing body that gets to me; a poignant contrast that reminds me of my mother, even when she was strong.

I've always been drawn to any story of a mother and a daughter on their own in the world. I saw *A Taste of Honey* several times as both a play and a film, and never stopped feeling it. Even *Gypsy* I saw over and over again, sneaking in backstage for the musical and going to the movies as well. I told myself that I was learning the tap-dance routines, but actually my eyes were full of tears.

I once fell in love with a man only because we both belonged to that large and secret club of children who had "crazy mothers." We traded stories of the shameful houses to which we could never invite our friends. Before he was born, his mother had gone to jail for her **pacifist**[18] convictions. Then she married the politically ambitious young lawyer who had defended her, stayed home and raised many sons. I fell out of love when he confessed that he wished I wouldn't smoke or swear, and he hoped I wouldn't go on working. His mother's plight had taught him self-pity—nothing else.

I'm no longer obsessed, as I was for many years, with the fear that I would end up in a house like that one in Toledo. Now, I'm obsessed instead with the things I could have done for my mother while she was alive, or the things I should have said.

---

[18] **pacifist**—nonviolent; opposition to war.

I still don't understand why so many, many years passed before I saw my mother as a person and before I understood that many of the forces in her life are patterns women share. Like a lot of daughters, I suppose I couldn't afford to admit that what had happened to my mother was not all personal or accidental, and therefore could happen to me.

One mystery has finally cleared. I could never understand why my mother hadn't been helped by Pauline, her mother-in-law; a woman she seemed to love more than her own mother. This paternal grandmother had died when I was five, before my mother's real problems began but long after that "nervous breakdown," and I knew Pauline was once a suffragist[19] who addressed Congress, marched for the vote, and was the first woman member of a school board in Ohio. She must have been a courageous and independent woman, yet I could find no evidence in my mother's reminiscences that Pauline had encouraged or helped my mother toward a life of her own.

I finally realized that my grandmother never changed the politics of her own life, either. She was a feminist who kept a neat house for a husband and four antifeminist sons, a vegetarian among five male meat eaters, and a woman who felt so strongly about the dangers of alcohol that she used only paste vanilla; yet she served both meat and wine to the men of the house and made sure their lives and comforts were continued undisturbed. After the vote was won, Pauline seems to have stopped all feminist activity. My mother greatly admired the fact that her mother-in-law kept a spotless house and prepared a week's meals at a time. Whatever her own internal torments, Pauline was to my mother a woman who seemed able to "do it all." "Whither thou goest, I shall go," my mother used to say to her much-loved mother-in-law,

---

[19] suffragist—one who fights for the right to vote, especially for women.

quoting the Ruth of the Bible.[20] In the end, her mother-in-law may have added to my mother's burdens of guilt.

Perhaps like many later suffragists, my grandmother was a public feminist and a private **isolationist**.[21] That may have been heroic in itself, the most she could be expected to do, but the vote and a legal right to work were not the only kind of help my mother needed.

The world still missed a unique person named Ruth. Though she longed to live in New York and in Europe, she became a woman who was afraid to take a bus across town. Though she drove the first Stanley Steamer, she married a man who never let her drive.

I can only guess what she might have become. The clues are in moments of spirit or humor.

After all the years of fear, she still came to Oberlin with me when I was giving a speech there. She remembered everything about its history as the first college to admit blacks and the first to admit women, and responded to students with the dignity of a professor, the accuracy of a journalist, and a charm that was all her own.

When she could still make trips to Washington's wealth of libraries, she became an expert genealogist,[22] delighting especially in finding the rogues and rebels in our family tree.

Just before I was born, when she had cooked one more enormous meal for all the members of some famous dance band at my father's resort and they failed to clean their plates, she had taken a shotgun down from the kitchen wall and held it over their frightened heads until they had finished the last crumb of strawberry shortcake. Only then did she tell them the gun wasn't loaded. It was a story she told with great satisfaction.

---

[20] Ruth of the Bible—Ruth was a widow who left home and followed her mother-in-law to Bethlehem.

[21] **isolationist**—one who prefers solitude over relationships or alliances with others.

[22] genealogist—person who studies one's family history.

Though sex was a subject she couldn't discuss directly, she had a great appreciation of sensuous men. When a friend I brought home tried to talk to her about cooking, she was furious. ("He came out in the kitchen and talked to me about *stew*!") But she forgave him when we went swimming. She whispered, "He has wonderful legs!"

On her seventy-fifth birthday, she played softball with her grandsons on the beach, and took pride in hitting home runs into the ocean.

Even in the last year of her life, when my sister took her to visit a neighbor's new and luxurious house, she looked at the vertical stripes of a very abstract painting in the hallway and said, tartly, "Is that the price code?"

She worried terribly about being socially accepted herself, but she never withheld her own approval for the wrong reasons. Poverty or style or lack of education couldn't stand between her and a new friend. Though she lived in a mostly white society and worried if I went out with a man of the "wrong" race, just as she had once married a man of the "wrong" religion, she always accepted each person as an individual.

"Is he *very* dark?" she once asked worriedly about a friend. But when she met this very dark person, she only said afterward, "What a kind and nice man!"

My father was the Jewish half of the family, yet it was my mother who taught me to have pride in that tradition. It was she who encouraged me to listen to a radio play about a concentration camp when I was little. "You should know that this can happen," she said. Yet she did it just enough to teach, never enough to frighten.

It was she who introduced me to books and a respect for them, to poetry that she knew by heart, and to the idea that you could never criticize someone unless you "walked miles in their shoes."

It was she who sold that Toledo house, the only home she had, with the determination that the money be used to start me in college. She gave both her daughters the encouragement to leave home for four years of independence that she herself had never had.

After her death, my sister and I found a journal she had kept of her one cherished and belated trip to Europe. It was a trip she had described very little when she came home: she always deplored people who talked boringly about their personal travels and showed slides. Nonetheless, she had written a descriptive essay called "Grandma Goes to Europe." She still must have thought of herself as a writer. Yet she showed this long journal to no one.

I miss her, but perhaps no more in death than I did in life. Dying seems less sad than having lived too little. But at least we're now asking questions about all the Ruths and all our family mysteries.

If her song inspires that, I think she would be the first to say: It was worth the singing.

QUESTIONS TO CONSIDER

1. What is the significance of the title of this essay?

2. How does Uncle Ed's life motivate Steinem both to unravel and to better understand the "mystery" of her mother's life? What essential differences does she see between how people responded to Uncle Ed's illness compared with reactions to her mother's illness?

3. When and how did Gloria Steinem begin to see her mother as someone she respected and could learn a great deal from? How was this possible, in your opinion, given the neglect that Gloria suffered during much of her childhood?

4. How do you think Steinem's experiences as a young girl led her to become a strong feminist and leader of the women's movement?

from

Breath, Eyes, Memory

BY EDWIDGE DANTICAT

Edwidge Danticat was born in Haiti in 1969. Her mother emigrated to the United States, leaving her to be raised by a devoted aunt. At the age of twelve, she came to America to join a mother she barely knew. After graduate school, she began to pursue her own writing. To date, Danticat has published numerous magazine articles, a collection of stories, Krik? Krak!, *and two novels,* Breath, Eyes, Memory, *and* The Farming of Bones. *She is the recipient of a James Michener fellowship, awards from* Seventeen *and* Essence *magazines, and the 1995 Women of Achievement Award. Jane magazine named her one of the "15 Gutsiest Women of the Year." She began writing* Breath, Eyes, Memory *(1994), excerpted here, when she was still in high school. It grew from an article to short stories and finally became a novel. The narrator, Sophie, has Danticat's keen eye and ear for detail, which enable her to communicate in details both large and small the issues facing a Haitian teenager as she moves toward independence.*

I was eighteen and going to start college in the fall. My mother continued working her two jobs, but she put in even longer hours. And we moved to a one-family house in a tree-lined neighborhood near where Marc[1] lived.

In the new place, my mother had a patch of land in the back where she started growing hibiscus. She had grown tired of daffodils.

We decorated our new living room in red, everything from the carpet to the plastic roses on the coffee table. I had my very own large bedroom with a new squeaky bed. My mother's room was even bigger, with a closet that you could have entertained some friends in. In some places in Haiti, her closet would have been a room on its own, and the clothes would not have bothered the fortunate child who would sleep in it.

Before the move, I had been going to a Haitian Adventist school that went from elementary right to high school. They had guaranteed my mother that they would get me into college and they had lived up to their pledge. Now my first classes at college were a few months away and my mother couldn't have been happier. Her sacrifices had paid off.

I never said this to my mother, but I hated the Maranatha Bilingual Institution. It was as if I had never left Haiti. All the lessons were in French,[2] except for English composition and literature classes. Outside the school, we were "the Frenchies," cringing in our mock-Catholic-school uniforms as the students from the public school across the street called us "boat people" and "stinking Haitians."

When my mother was home, she made me read out loud from the English Composition textbooks. The first English words I read sounded like rocks falling in a stream. Then very slowly things began to take on some meaning. There were words that I heard often. Words

---

[1] Marc—the boyfriend of Sophie's mother, who is also Haitian.

[2] French is the language of government and business in Haiti.

that jump out of New York Creole[3] conversations, like the last kernel in a cooling popcorn machine. Words, among others, like *TV, building, feeling*, which Marc and my mother used even when they were in the middle of a heated political discussion in Creole. *Mwin gin yon feeling. I have a feeling Haiti will get back on its feet one day, but I'll be dead before it happens*. My mother, always the pessimist.

There were other words that helped too, words that looked almost the same in French, but were pronounced differently in English: *nationality, alien, race, enemy, date, present*. These and other words gave me a context for the rest that I did not understand.

Eventually, I began to hear myself that I read better. I answered swiftly when my mother asked me a question in English. Not that I ever had a chance to show it off at school, but I became an English speaker.

"There is great responsibility that comes with knowledge," my mother would say. My great responsibility was to study hard. I spent six years doing nothing but that. School, home, and prayer.

Tante Atie[4] once said that love is like rain. It comes in a drizzle sometimes. Then it starts pouring and if you're not careful it will drown you.

I was eighteen and I fell in love. His name was Joseph and he was old. He was old like God is old to me, ever present and full of wisdom.

He looked somewhat like Monsieur Augustin.[5] He was the color of ground coffee, with a cropped beard and a voice like molasses that turned to music when he held a saxophone to his lips.

He broke the monotony of my shuffle between home and school when he moved into the empty house next door to ours.

---

[3] Creole—the vernacular or common language spoken in the home and neighborhood in Haiti, based on French and English.

[4] Tante Atie—Sophie's Aunt Atie, with whom she lived in Haiti before she moved to the United States.

[5] Monsieur Augustin—one of Sophie's old neighbors from Haiti.

My mother never trusted him. In the back of my mind echoed her constant warning, "You keep away from those American boys." The ones whose eyes followed me on the street. The ones who were supposedly drooling over me afterwards, even though they called me a nasty West Indian to my face. "You keep away from them especially. They are upset because they cannot have you."

Aside from Marc, we knew no other men. Men were as mysterious to me as white people, who in Haiti we had only known as missionaries. I tried to imagine my mother's reaction to Joseph. I could already hear her: "Not if he were the last unmarried man on earth."

When she came home during the day and saw him sitting on his porch steps next door, she would nod a quick hello and walk faster. She wrapped her arms tighter around me, as though to rescue me from his stare.

Somehow, early on, I felt that he might like me. The way his eyes trailed me up the block gave him away. My mother liked to say, "I admire priests because they like women for more than their faces and their buttocks." Joseph's look went beyond the face and the buttocks.

He looked like the kind of man who could buy a girl a meal without asking for her bra in return.

Whenever I went by his **stoop**,[6] I felt like we were conspiring. How could I smile without my mother noticing and how could he respond to her brisk hello and mine too, without letting her see that wink that was for me alone?

At night, I fantasized that he was sitting somewhere pining away, dreaming about me, thinking of a way to enter my life. Then one day, like rain, he came to my front door.

I was stretched out on the couch with a chemistry book when I heard the knock. I looked through the security peephole to check. It was him.

---

[6] **stoop**—front porch; front step.

"Can I use your phone?" he asked. "I've had mine disconnected because I'm going out of town soon."

I opened the door and led him to the phone. Our fingers touched as I handed it to him. He dialed quickly, smiling with his eyes on my face.

"Did we get it?" he asked into the phone.

His feet bounced off the ground when he heard the answer. "Yes!" he shouted. "Yes!"

He handed me back the phone with a wink.

"Have you ever really wanted something great and gotten it?" he asked.

My face must have been blank.

He asked me the question again, then suddenly slapped his forehead.

"I haven't even introduced myself."

"My name is Sophie," I said, jumping ahead.

"I am Joseph," he said. I knew.

"Was it good news you just got?"

"What gave me away?"

He looked at me as though he was waiting for me to say something equally witty. I wasn't as **glib**,[7] as fast on my feet. I couldn't think of anything.

"It *was* good news," he answered. "I just found out that we got a gig in the East Village from now until our tour starts."

"A gig?"

"A job. I am a musician."

"I know," I said. "Sometimes I hear you playing at night."

"Does it bother you?"

"*Non*, it's very pretty."

"I detect an accent," he said.

Oh please, say a small one, I thought. After seven years in this country, I was tired of having people detect

---

[7] **glib**—quick and comfortable in conversation.

my accent. I wanted to sound completely American, especially for him.

"Where are you from?" he asked.

"Haiti."

"Ah," he said, "I have never been there. Do you speak Creole?"

"*Oui, Oui,*" I ventured, for a laugh.

"We, we," he said, pointing to me and him. "We have something in common. *Mwin aussi.* I speak a form of Creole, too. I am from Louisiana. My parents considered themselves what we call Creoles. Is it a small world or what?"

I shook my head yes. It was a very small world.

"You live alone?" he asked.

My mother's constant suspicion prodded me and I quickly said, "No." Just in case he was thinking of coming over tonight to kill me. This was New York, after all. You could not trust anybody.

"I live with my mother."

"I have seen her," he said.

"She works."

"Nights?"

"Sometimes."

"Did you two just move here?"

"Yes, we did."

"I thought so," he said. "Whenever I'm in New York, I sublet[8] in the neighborhood and I have never seen you walking around before."

"We moved about a year ago."

"That's about the last time I was in Brooklyn."

"Where are you the rest of the year?"

"In Providence."

I was immediately fascinated by the name. Providence. Fate! A town named for the Creator, the Almighty. Who would not want to live there?

---

[8] sublet—rent property from a person who has leased it, rather than from the owner.

"I am away from my house about six months out of the year," he said. "I travel to different places with my band and then after a while I go back for some peace and quiet."

"What is it like in Providence?" I asked.

"It is calm. I can drive to the river and watch the sun set. I think you would like it there. You seem like a deep, thoughtful kind of person."

"I am."

"I like that in people. I like that very much."

He glanced down at his feet as though he couldn't think of anything else to say.

I wanted to ask him to stay, but my mother would be home soon.

"I work at home," he finally said, "in case you ever want to drop by."

I spent the whole week with my ear pressed against the wall, listening to him rehearse. He rehearsed day and night, sometimes twelve to ten hours without stopping. Sometimes at night, the saxophone was like a soothing lullaby.

One afternoon, he came by with a ham-and-cheese sandwich to thank me for letting him use the phone. He sat across from me in the living room while I ate very slowly.

"What are you going to study in college?" he asked.

"I think I am going to be a doctor."

"You *think*? Is this something you like?"

"I suppose so," I said.

"You have to have a passion for what you do."

"My mother says it's important for us to have a doctor in the family."

"What if you don't want to be a doctor?"

"There's a difference between what a person wants and what's good for them."

"You sound like you are quoting someone," he said.

"My mother."

"What would Sophie like to do?" he asked.

That was the problem. Sophie really wasn't sure. I had never really dared to dream on my own.

"You're not sure, are you?"

He even understood my silences.

"It is okay not to have your future on a map," he said. "That way you can flow wherever life takes you."

"That is not Haitian," I said. "That's very American."

"What is?"

"Being a wanderer. The very idea."

"I am not American," he said. "I am African American."

"What is the difference?"

"The African. It means that you and I, we are already part of each other."

I think I blushed. At least I nearly choked on my sandwich. He walked over and tapped my back.

"Are you all right?"

"I am fine," I said, still short of breath.

"I think you are a fine woman," he said.

I started choking again.

I knew what my mother would think of my going over there during the day. A good girl would never be alone with a man, an older one at that. I wasn't thinking straight. It was nice waking up in the morning knowing I had someone to talk to.

I started going next door every day. The living room was bare except for a couch and a few boxes packed in a corner near his synthesizer and loud speakers.

At first I would sit on the linoleum and listen to him play. Then slowly, I moved closer until sometimes he would let me touch the keyboard, guiding my fingers with his hand on top of mine.

Between strokes, I learned the story of his life. He was from a middle-class New Orleans family. His parents died when he was young. He was on his own by the time he was fifteen. He went to college in Providence but by his sophomore year left school and bought a house there. He was lucky he had been left enough money to pursue his dream of being a musician. He liked to play slave songs, Negro spirituals, both on his saxophone and his piano, slowing them down or speeding them up at different tempos. One day, he would move back to Providence for good, and write his own songs.

QUESTIONS TO CONSIDER

1. What are the major issues Sophie faces in growing up?

2. How does Sophie seem to feel about being Haitian?

3. What does Joseph contribute to Sophie's understanding of herself and her identity?

4. What does Sophie's mother contribute? In what ways does her mother help her to develop? In what ways do Sophie's mother's actions and attitudes conflict with the ways that Sophie wants to grow up?

La Gringuita

BY JULIA ALVAREZ

Julia Alvarez (1950–　) came to the United States from the Dominican Republic as a young teenager. She explores the themes of loss of native land, language, culture, and extended family in her works, including How the Garcia Girls Lost Their Accents, In the Time of Butterflies, *a National Book Critics Circle Award finalist, and* Yo!. *The selection here is from* Something to Declare *(1998), a collection of essays and reminiscences. In it, Alvarez describes the effect of language and culture in defining the woman she would become.*

The inevitable, of course, has happened. I now speak my native language "with an accent." What I mean by this is that I speak perfect childhood Spanish, but if I stray into a heated discussion or complex explanation, I have to ask, "Por favor ¿Puedo decirlo en inglés?" Can I please say it in English?

How and why did this happen?

When we emigrated to the United States in the early sixties, the climate was not favorable for retaining our Spanish. I remember one scene in a grocery store soon after we arrived. An elderly shopper, overhearing my mother speaking Spanish to her daughters, muttered that if we wanted to be in this country, we should learn the language. "I do know the language," my mother said in her boarding-school English, putting the woman in her place. She knew the value of speaking perfect English. She had studied for several years at Abbot Academy, flying up from the Island to New York City, and then taking the train up to Boston. It was during the war, and the train would sometimes fill with servicemen, every seat taken.

One time, a young sailor asked my mother if he could sit in the empty seat beside her and chew on her ear. My mother gave him an indignant look, stood up, and went in search of the conductor to report this fresh man. Decades later, hearing the story, my father, ever vigilant and jealous of his wife and daughters, was convinced—no matter what my mother said about **idiomatic**[1] expressions—that the sailor had made an advance. He, himself, was never comfortable in English. In fact, if there were phone calls to be made to billing offices, medical supply stores, Workman's Compensation, my father would put my mother on the phone. She would get better results than he would with his heavy, almost incomprehensible accent.

At school, there were several incidents of name-calling and stone-throwing, which our teachers claimed would stop if my sisters and I joined in with the other kids and quit congregating together at recess and jabbering away in Spanish. Those were the days before bilingual education or multicultural studies, when kids like us were thrown in the deep end of the public school pool and left to fend for ourselves. Not everyone came up for air.

---

[1] **idiomatic**—like an idiom, an expression that has a meaning different from the literal meaning of its words. To "chew on her ear" is an idiomatic expression that means to have a conversation.

Mami managed to get us scholarships to her old boarding school where Good Manners and Tolerance and English Skills were required. We were also all required to study a foreign language, but my teachers talked me into taking French. In fact, they felt my studying Spanish was equivalent to my taking a "gut course." Spanish was my native tongue, after all, a language I already had in the bag and would always be able to speak whenever I wanted. Meanwhile, with Saturday drills and daily writing assignments, our English skills soon met school requirements. By the time my sisters and I came home for vacations, we were rolling our eyes in exasperation at our old-world Mami and Papi, using expressions like *far out*, and *what a riot!* and *outta sight*, and *believe you me* as if we had been born to them.

As rebellious adolescents, we soon figured out that conducting our **filial**[2] business in English gave us an edge over our strict, Spanish-speaking parents. We could spin circles around my mother's *absolutamante no* by pointing out the flaws in her arguments, in English. My father was a pushover for **pithy**[3] quotes from Shakespeare, and a recitation of "The quality of mercy is not strained" could usually get me what I wanted. Usually. There were areas we couldn't touch even with a Shakespearean ten-foot pole: the area of boys and permission to go places where there might be boys, American boys, with their mouths full of bubblegum and their minds full of the devil.

Our growing distance from Spanish was a way in which we were setting ourselves free from that old world where, as girls, we didn't have much say about what we could do with our lives. In English, we didn't have to use the formal *usted*[4] that immediately put us in

---

[2] **filial**—parent-child relationship.

[3] **pithy**—meaty, significant.

[4] *usted*—"you," formal. In Spanish, the speaker must decide whether to use formal or informal constructions. When a child addresses a parent or adult, he or she uses the formal construction. Parents would use an informal construction in response.

our place with our elders. We were responsible for ourselves and that made us feel grown-up. We couldn't just skirt culpability[5] by using the reflexive:[6] the bag of cookies did not finish itself, nor did the money disappear itself from Mami's purse. We had no one to bail us out of American trouble once we went our own way in English. No family connections, no tío[7] whose name might open doors for us. If the world was suddenly less friendly, it was also more exciting. We found out we could do things we had never done before. We could go places in English we never could in Spanish, if we put our minds to it. And we put our combined four minds to it, believe you me.

My parents, anxious that we not lose our tie to our native land, and no doubt thinking of future husbands for their four daughters, began sending us "home" every summer to Mami's family in the capital. And just as we had once huddled in the school playground, speaking Spanish for the comfort of it, my sisters and I now hung out together in "the D.R.,"[8] as we referred to it, kibitzing[9] in English on the crazy world around us: the silly rules for girls, the obnoxious behavior of macho guys, the deplorable situation of the poor. My aunts and uncles tried unsuccessfully to stem this tide of our Americanization, whose main expression was, of course, our use of the English language. "Tienen que hablar en español,"[10] they commanded. "Ay, come on," we would say as if we had been asked to go back to baby talk as grown-ups.

By now, we couldn't go back as easily as that. Our Spanish was full of English. Countless times during a

---

[5] skirt culpability—avoid blame.

[6] reflexive—in Spanish, sentences are frequently constructed with reflexive verbs, so that they are passively constructed. In these sentences, there is no subject who performs the action.

[7] tío—uncle.

[8] D.R.—Dominican Republic.

[9] kibitzing—gossiping.

[10] "Tienen que hablar en español."—"They have to speak in Spanish."

conversation, we were corrected, until what we had to say was lost in our saying it wrong. More and more we chose to answer in English even when the question was posed in Spanish. It was a measure of the growing distance between ourselves and our native culture—a distance we all felt we could easily retrace with just a little practice. It wasn't until I failed at first love, in Spanish, that I realized how unbridgeable that gap had become.

That summer I went down to the Island by myself. My sisters had chosen to stay in the States at a summer camp where the oldest was a counselor. But I was talked into going "home" by my father, whose nephew—an older (by twenty years) cousin of mine—had been elected the president of El Centro de Recreo, the social club of his native town of Santiago. Every year at El Centro, young girls of fifteen were "presented" in public, a little like a debutante ball. I was two years past the deadline, but I had a baby face and could easily pass for five years younger than I was—something I did not like to hear. And my father very much wanted for one of his daughters to represent la familia among the crème de la crème[11] of his hometown society.

I arrived with my DO-YOUR-OWN-THING!!! T-shirt and bell-bottom pants and several novels by Herman Hesse, ready to spread the seeds of the sixties revolution raging in the States. Unlike other visits with my bilingual cousins in the capital, this time I was staying in a sleepy, old-fashioned town in the interior with Papi's side of the family, none of whom spoke English.

Actually I wasn't even staying in town. Cousin Utcho, whom I called *tío* because he was so much older than I was, and his wife, Betty—who, despite her name, didn't speak a word of English either—lived far out in the countryside on a large chicken farm where he was the foreman. They treated me like a ten-year-old, or so I thought, monitoring phone calls, not allowing male

---

[11] crème de la crème—very best.

visitors, explaining their carefulness by reminding me that my parents had entrusted them with my person and they wanted to return me in the same condition in which I had arrived. Out there in the boonies, the old-world traditions had been preserved full strength. But I can't help thinking that in part, Utcho and Betty treated me like a ten-year-old because I talked like a ten-year-old in my halting, childhood Spanish. I couldn't explain about women's liberation and the quality of mercy not being strained, in Spanish. I grew bored and lonely, and was ready to go back to New York and call it quits on being "presented," when I met Dilita.

Like me, Dilita was a **hybrid**.[12] Her parents had moved to Puerto Rico when she was three, and she had lived for some time with a relative in New York. But her revolutionary zeal had taken the turn of glamour girl rather than my New England-hippy variety. In fact, Dilita looked just like the other Dominican girls. She had a teased hairdo; I let my long hair hang loose in a style I can only describe as "blowing in the wind." Dilita wore makeup; I did a little lipstick and maybe eyeliner if she would put it on for me. She wore outfits; I had peasant blouses, T-shirts, and blue jeans.

But in one key way, Dilita was more of a rebel than I was: she did exactly what she wanted without guilt or apology. She was in charge of her own destino,[13] as she liked to say, and no one was going to talk her into giving that up. I was in awe of Dilita. She was the first "hyphenated" person[14] I had ever met whom I considered successful, not tortured as a hybrid the way my sisters and I were.

Dilita managed to talk Utcho into letting me move into town with her and her young, married aunt,

---

[12] **hybrid**—of mixed origin.

[13] destino—destiny; fate.

[14] "hyphenated" person—citizen of the United States whose origin is shown in hyphenated words, as in German-American, Mexican-American.

Carmen. Mamacán, as we called her, was liberal and lighthearted and gave us free rein to do what we wanted. "Just as long as you girls don't get in trouble!" Trouble came in one **denomination**,[15] we knew, and neither of us were fools. When the matrons in town complained about our miniskirts or about our driving around with boys and no chaperons, Mamacán threw up her hands and said, "¡Pero si son americanas!" They're American girls!

We hit it off with the boys. All the other girls came with their mamis or tías in tow; Dilita and I were free and clear. Inside of a week we both had boyfriends. Dilita, who was prettier than I, landed the handsome tipo,[16] tall Eladio with raven-black hair and arched eyebrows and the arrogant stance of a flamenco dancer, whereas I ended up with his chubby sidekick, a honey-skinned young man with wonderful dimples and a pot belly that made him look like a Dominican version of the Pillsbury doughboy. His name was Manuel Gustavo, but I affectionately nicknamed him Mangú, after a mashed plantain dish that is a staple of Dominican diet. A few days after meeting him, Mangú's mother sent over an elaborate dessert with lots of white frosting that looked suggestively like a wedding cake. "Hint hint," Dilita joked, an expression everyone was using at her school, too.

Every night the four of us went out together: Dilita sat up front with Eladio, who had his own car, and I in the backseat with Mangú—a very cozy boy-girl arrangement. But actually, if anyone had been listening in on these dates, they would have thought two American girlfriends were out for a whirl around the town. Dilita and I yakked, back and forth, starting first in Spanish out of consideration for our boyfriends, but switching over into English as we got more involved in whatever we

---

[15] **denomination**—category.

[16] tipo—guy.

were talking about. Every once in a while, one of the guys would ask us, "¿Y qué lo que ustedes tanto hablan?" For some reason, this request to know what we were talking about would give us both an attack of giggles. Sometimes, Eladio, with Mangú joining in, sang the lyrics of a popular song to let us know we were being obnoxious:

> Las hijas de Juan Mejía
> son bonitas y bailan bien
> pero tienen un defecto
> que se rien de to' el que ven.

> (The daughters of Juan Mejía
> dance well and are so pretty
> but they've got one bad quality,
> they make fun of everybody.)

Las gringuitas, they nicknamed us. Delita didn't mind the teasing, but Mangú could always get a rise out of me when he called me a gringa.[17] Perhaps, just a few years away from the name-calling my sisters and I had experienced on the school playground, I felt instantly defensive whenever anyone tried to pin me down with a label.

But though he teased me with that nickname, Mangú made it clear that he would find a real gringa unappealing. "You're Dominican," he declared. The **litmus test**[18] was dancing merengue, our national, fast-moving, lots-of-hip-action dance. As we moved across the dance floor, Mangú would whisper the lyrics in my ear, complimenting my natural rhythm that showed, so he said, that my body knew where it came from. I was pleased with the praise. The truth is I wanted it both ways: I wanted to be good at the best things in each culture. Maybe I was picking up from Dilita how to be a successful hybrid.

---

[17] gringa—disparaging term for a female Spanish-American.
[18] **litmus test**—crucial test in which one factor is decisive.

Still, when I tried to talk to Mangú about something of substance, the conversation foundered. I couldn't carry on in Spanish about complicated subjects, and Mangú didn't know a word of English. Our silences troubled me. Maybe my tías were right. Too much education in English could spoil a girl's chances in Spanish.

But at least I had Dilita to talk to about how confusing it all was. "You and I," she often told me as we lay under the mosquito net in the big double bed Mamacán had fixed for us, "we have the best of both worlds. We can have a good time here, and we can have a good time there."

"Yeah," I'd say, not totally convinced.

Down on the street, every Saturday night, the little conjunto[19] that Eladio and Mangú had hired would serenade us with romantic canciones.[20] We were not supposed to show our faces, but Dilita and I always snuck out on the balcony in our baby dolls[21] to talk to the guys. Looking down at Mangú from above, I could see the stiffness of the white dress shirt his mother had starched and ironed for him. I felt a pang of tenderness and regret. What was wrong with me, I wondered, that I wasn't falling in love with him?

After the presentation ball, Dilita left for Puerto Rico to attend a cousin's wedding. It was then, when I was left alone with Manuel Gustavo, that I realized that the problem was not me, but me *and* Manuel Gustavo.

Rather than move back to the lonely boonies, I stayed on in town with Dilita's aunt for the two weeks remaining of my visit. But without Dilita, town life was as lonely as life on a chicken farm. Evenings, Mangú would come over, and we'd sit on the patio and try to make conversation or drive out to the country club in a

---

[19] conjunto—group.

[20] canciones—songs.

[21] baby dolls—pajamas. Popular in the 1960s, baby doll pajamas were characterized by short pants and lots of lace.

borrowed car to dance merengue and see what everyone else was doing. What *we* were doing was looking for people to fill up our silence with their talk.

One night, Mangú drove out towards Utcho's chicken farm and pulled over at a spot where often the four of us had stopped to look at the stars. We got out of the car and leaned against the side, enjoying the breeze. In the dark, periodically broken by the lights of passing cars, Mangú began to talk about our future.

I didn't know what to say to him. Or actually, in English, I could have said half a dozen **ambivalent**,[22] soothing things. But not having a complicated vocabulary in Spanish, I didn't know the fancy, smooth-talking ways of delaying and deterring. Like a child, I could just blurt out what I was thinking.

"Somos diferente, Mangú." We are so different. The comment came out sounding inane.

"No, we're not," he argued back. "We're both Dominicans. Our families come from the same hometown."

"But we left," I said, looking up at the stars. From this tropical perspective, the stars seemed to form different constellations in the night sky. Even the Big Dipper, which was so easy to spot in New England, seemed to be misplaced here. Tonight, it lay on its side, right above us. I was going to point it out to Mangú—in part to distract him, but I could not remember the word for *dipper*—la cuchara grande, the big spoon?

But Mangú would not have been interested in the stars anyway. Once it was clear that we did not share the same feelings, there was nothing much left to say. We drove back to Mamacán's house in silence.

I don't know if that experience made Mangú forever wary with half-breed Dominican-York girls; *gringuitas*, who seemed to be talking out of both sides of their

---

[22] **ambivalent**—uncertain, indecisive.

mouths, and in two different languages, to boot. I myself never had a Spanish-only boyfriend again. Maybe the opportunity never presented itself, or maybe it was that as English became my dominant tongue, too many parts of me were left out in Spanish for me to be able to be intimate with a potential life partner in only that language.

Still, the yearning remained. How wonderful to love someone whose skin was the same honey-dipped, sallow-based color; who said *concho*[23] when he was mad and *cielito lindo*[24] when he wanted to butter you up! "¡Ay! to make love in Spanish . . .," the Latina narrator of Sandra Cisneros's story, "Bien Pretty," exclaims. "To have a lover whisper things in that language crooned to babies, that language murmured by grandmothers, those words that smelled like your house . . .." But I wonder if after the Latina **protagonist**[25] makes love with her novio,[26] she doesn't sit up in bed and tell him the story of her life in English with a few palabritas[27] thrown in to capture the rhythm of her Latin heartbeat?

As for Manuel Gustavo, I met up with him a few years ago on a visit to the Island. My husband, a gringo from Nebraska, and I were driving down the two-lane *autopista*[28] on our way up to the mountains on a land search. A pickup roared past us. Suddenly, it slowed and pulled onto the shoulder. As we drove by, the driver started honking. "What does he want me to do?" my husband shouted at me. I looked over and saw that the driver was still on the shoulder, trying to catch up with us. I gestured, what do you want?

"Soy yo," the man called out, "Manuel Gustavo."

---

[23] *concho*—a derogatory term for a woman.

[24] *cielito lindo*—heavenly, angel; literally, beautiful sky.

[25] **protagonist**—main character in a story.

[26] novio—sweetheart.

[27] palabritas—little Spanish words.

[28] *autopista*—freeway.

Almost thirty years had passed. He had gotten heavier; his hairline had receded; there was gray in his hair. But the dimples were still there. Beside him sat a boy about seven or eight, a young duplicate of the boy I had known. "Mangú!" I called out. "Is that really you?"

By this time my husband was angry at the insanity of this pick-up trying to keep up with us on the narrow shoulder while Mack trucks roared by on the other lane. "Tell him we'll stop ahead, and you guys can talk!"

But the truth was that I didn't want to stop and talk to Manuel Gustavo. What would I have said to him now, when I hadn't been able to talk to him thirty years ago? "It's good to see you again, Mangú," I shouted. I waved good-bye as my husband pulled ahead. In my side mirror, I watched as he signaled, then disappeared into the long line of traffic behind us.

"Who was that?" my husband wanted to know.

I went on to tell my husband the story of that summer: the presentation; Utcho and Betty; my worldly-wise friend Dilita; Eladio, who looked like a flamenco dancer; the serenades; the big double bed Dilita and I slept in with a mosquito net tied to the four posts. And of course, I told him the story of my romance with Manuel Gustavo.

And, as I spoke, that old yearning came back. What would my life have been like if I had stayed in my native country? The truth was I couldn't even imagine myself as someone other than the person I had become in English, a woman who writes books in the language of Emily Dickinson and Walt Whitman, and also of the rude shopper in the grocery store and of the boys throwing stones in the schoolyard, their language, which is now my language. A woman who has joined her life with the life of a man who grew up on a farm in Nebraska, whose great-grandparents came over from Germany and discouraged their own children from speaking German because of the **antipathy**[29] that erupted in their new country towards anything German with the outbreak of World War I. A woman who is now looking for land in the Dominican Republic with her husband, so that they can begin to spend some time in the land she came from.

When we took the turnoff into the mountains, we rolled up our windows so we could easily hear the cassette player. My husband had ordered Spanish-language tapes a while back from the Foreign Service Institute so that he could keep up with my family in the capital. Recently, he had dusted them off and started listening to them to prepare himself for our land hunt. I had decided to join him in these lessons, in part to encourage him, but also because I wanted to regain the language that would allow me to feel at home again in my native country.

---

[29] **antipathy**—dislike.

QUESTIONS TO CONSIDER

1. What advantages did Julia have as an American girl living in the Dominican Republic for the summer? What disadvantages did she experience?

2. How did speaking English instead of Spanish change the attitudes of Julia and her sisters?

3. What were the differences between the ways Dominican and American girls were expected to behave?

Authors

▲
Gloria Steinem (left) shaking hands with President Jimmy Carter

▲
Elizabeth Cady Stanton

Betty Friedan ▶

▲
Amelia Earhart

Julia Alvarez ▶

▲
Edwidge Danticat

▲
Eudora Welty

▲
Sandra Jackson-Opoku

▲
Danzy Senna

▲
Nellie Wong

Riding the Whirlwind:
Rebel Women

Movin' and Steppin'

BY AKASHA (GLORIA) HULL

In a sense, all feminists are "rebel women" because they challenge society's accepted truths about the role of women. Akasha Hull is an African-American scholar, poet, and feminist. In 1982 she co-authored All the Women Are White, All the Blacks Are Men: But Some of Us Are Brave, *a women's studies anthology on the history of black feminist thought. Hull is currently a professor of women's studies and literature at the University of California at Santa Cruz. Her literary criticism and poetry have appeared in numerous journals, including* Black American Literature Forum, Chrysalis, *and* Obsidian. *In the following poem, which flows with a rhythm suggested in the title, Hull challenges women to take the risk of redefining and reinventing themselves.*

There are times when
one needs to move—
to newer places
wider spaces

      exchange the pond
      for the ocean
      and jump right in
      (it don't matter if your hair gets wet or **briny**)[1]

Mothers can tell you
shoes get too tight
and clothes grow old

How can you be Cinderella
      in the same tired frumpy frog gown
let alone Nerfertiti or Cleopatra[2]
      conquering the Nile

It just won't do.

Generally speaking,
it's hard for people's eyes
      to readjust
There you stand—
      a brand new *thang*
and they keep talking to someone
      you left behind long time ago
(and swear you never want to see again)

---

[1] **briny**—salty; filled with sea water.

[2] Nerfertiti or Cleopatra—queens of Ancient Egypt, both noted for great beauty.

Jive action like that
can push you back—
into the Dark Ages, a closet,
some fancy trickbag or **claustrophobic**[3] hole
Take a stroll
down different streets
where there are flowers that you can't name
and sights you've never seen before
Where the air breathes fresher
                    and people take you for a stranger

And you can keep on walking
hightime stepping getting up walking
into that future self
you got to be

---

[3] **claustrophobic**—fearfully closed in, narrow space.

QUESTIONS TO CONSIDER

1. What does Hull mean by "exchange the pond for the ocean"?

2. What do the tight shoes, old clothes, and "frumpy frog gown" stand for?

3. Why is it hard for people's eyes to "readjust" to changes a friend or family member might make? What does the author caution can happen if people don't recognize the new self?

4. What can the "different streets" add to the process of defining oneself?

5. Does the writer see the process of redefining oneself as a polite, gentle process, or in general is another kind of energy called for? How do you think Hull would define the "whirlwind" of being a rebel woman?

The Homesteader's Marriage and a Little Funeral

BY ELINORE PRUITT STEWART

Born in 1878, Elinore Pruitt Stewart homesteaded in Wyoming starting in 1909. After losing her husband in a railroad accident, she took her two-year-old daughter Jerrine and went to Denver in search of employment. After working as a housecleaner and laundress, she became the housekeeper for a cattleman, Mr. Clyde Stewart, in Wyoming. In the following letter, written in 1912 to her former employer in Denver, Stewart explains how she came to give up her plan to "knock about footloose and free." The letter is from her book, Letters of a Woman Homesteader *(1914).*

December 2, 1912

DEAR MRS. CONEY,—

Every time I get a new letter from you I get a new inspiration, and I am always glad to hear from you.

I have often wished I might tell you all about my Clyde, but have not because of two things. One is I could not even begin without telling you what a good man he is, and I didn't want you to think I could do nothing but brag. The other reason is the haste I married in. I am ashamed of that. I am afraid you will think me a Becky Sharp[1] of a person. But although I married in haste, I have no cause to repent. That is very fortunate because I have never had one bit of leisure to repent in. So I am lucky all around. The engagement was powerfully short because both agreed that the trend of events and ranch work seemed to require that we be married first and do our "sparking" afterward. You see, we had to chink in the wedding between times, that is, between planting the oats and other work that must be done early or not at all. In Wyoming ranchers can scarcely take time even to be married in the springtime. That having been settled, the license was sent for by mail, and as soon as it came Mr. Stewart saddled Chub and went down to the house of Mr. Pearson, the justice of the peace and a friend of long standing. I had never met any of the family and naturally rather dreaded to have them come, but Mr. Stewart was firm in wanting to be married at home, so he told Mr. Pearson he wanted him and his family to come up the following Wednesday and serve papers on the "wooman i' the hoose."[2] They were astonished, of course, but being such good friends they promised him all the assistance they could render. They are quite the dearest, most interesting family! I have since learned to love them as my own.

Well, there was no time to make wedding clothes, so I had to "do up" what I did have. Isn't it queer how sometimes, do what you can, work will keep getting in the way until you can't get anything done? That is how it was with me those few days before the wedding; so

---

[1] Becky Sharp—the selfish, clever, ambitious heroine of Thackeray's 1848 novel, *Vanity Fair*.

[2] "wooman i the hoose"—woman in the house, in Scottish dialect.

much so that when Wednesday dawned everything was topsy-turvy and I had a very strong desire to run away. But I always did hate a "piker,"[3] so I stood pat. Well, I had most of the dinner cooked, but it kept me hustling to get the house into anything like decent order before the old dog barked, and I knew my moments of liberty were limited. It was blowing a perfect hurricane and snowing like midwinter. I had bought a beautiful pair of shoes to wear on that day, but my vanity had squeezed my feet a little, so while I was so busy at work I had kept on a worn old pair, intending to put on the new ones later; but when the Pearsons drove up all I thought about was getting them into the house where there was fire, so I forgot all about the old shoes and the apron I wore.

I had only been here six weeks then, and was a stranger. That is why I had no one to help me and was so confused and hurried. As soon as the newcomers were warm, Mr. Stewart told me I had better come over by him and stand up. It was a large room I had to cross, and how I did it before all those strange eyes I never knew. All I can remember very distinctly is hearing Mr. Stewart saying, "I will," and myself chiming in that I would, too. Happening to glance down, I saw that I had forgotten to take off my apron or my old shoes, but just then Mr. Pearson pronounced us man and wife, and as I had dinner to serve right away I had no time to worry over my odd toilet.[4] Anyway the shoes were comfortable and the apron white, so I suppose it could have been worse; and I don't think it has ever made any difference with the Pearsons, for I number them all among my most **esteemed**[5] friends.

It is customary here for newlyweds to give a dance and supper at the hall, but as I was a stranger I preferred

---

[3] "piker"—person who picks up and leaves abruptly.

[4] my odd toilet—archaic phrase meaning, in this case, the strange way she is dressed and groomed.

[5] **esteemed**—highly regarded.

not to, and so it was a long time before I became acquainted with all my neighbors. I had not thought I should ever marry again. Jerrine was always such a dear little pal, and I wanted to just knock about foot-loose and free to see life as a gypsy sees it. I had planned to see the Cliff-Dwellers' home; to live right there until I caught the spirit of the surroundings enough to live over their lives in imagination anyway. I had planned to see the old missions and to go to Alaska; to hunt in Canada. I even dreamed of Honolulu. Life stretched out before me one long, happy **jaunt**.[6] I aimed to see all the world I could, but to travel unknown bypaths to do it. But first I wanted to try homesteading.

But for my having the grippe,[7] I should never have come to Wyoming. Mrs. Seroise, who was a nurse at the institution for nurses in Denver while I was housekeeper there, had worked one summer at Saratoga, Wyoming. It was she who told me of the pine forests. I had never seen a pine until I came to Colorado; so the idea of a home among the pines fascinated me. At that time I was hoping to pass the Civil-Service examination, with no very definite idea as to what I would do, but just to be improving my time and opportunity. I never went to a public school a day in my life. In my childhood days there was no such thing in the Indian Territory part of Oklahoma where we lived, so I have had to try hard to keep learning. Before the time came for the examination I was so discouraged because of the grippe that nothing but the mountains, the pines, and the clean, fresh air seemed worth while; so it all came about just as I have written you.

So you see I was very deceitful. Do you remember, I wrote you of a little baby boy dying? That was my own little Jamie, our first little son. For a long time my heart was crushed. He was such a sweet, beautiful boy.

---

[6] **jaunt**—pleasurable excursion.

[7] grippe—an acute virus much like influenza.

I wanted him so much. He died of erysipelas.[8] I held him in my arms till the last agony was over. Then I dressed the beautiful little body for the grave. Clyde is a carpenter; so I wanted him to make the little coffin. He did it every bit, and I lined and padded it, trimmed and covered it. Not that we couldn't afford to buy one or that our neighbors were not all that was kind and willing; but because it was a sad pleasure to do everything for our little first-born ourselves.

As there had been no physician to help, so there was no minister to comfort, and I could not bear to let our baby leave the world without leaving any message to a community that sadly needed it. His little message to us had been love, so I selected a chapter from John[9] and we had a funeral service, at which all our neighbors for thirty miles around were present. So you see, our union is sealed by love and **welded**[10] by a great sorrow.

Little Jamie was the first little Stewart. God has given me two more precious little sons. The old sorrow is not so keen now. I can bear to tell you about it, but I never could before. When you think of me you must think of me as one who is truly happy. It is true, I want a great many things I haven't got, but I don't want them enough to be discontented and not enjoy the many blessings that are mine. I have my home among the blue mountains, my healthy, well-formed children, my clean, honest husband, my kind, gentle milk cows, my garden which I make myself. I have loads and loads of flowers which I tend myself. There are lots of chickens, turkeys, and pigs which are my own special care. I have some slow old gentle horses and an old wagon. I can load up the kiddies and go where I please any time. I have the best, kindest neighbors and I have my dear absent friends. Do you wonder I am so happy? When

---

[8] erysipelas—a contagious infection of the skin and underlying tissue which causes the affected areas to turn red and swell. Today it is rather mild and clears up rapidly when penicillin or other antibiotics are taken.

[9] from John—from the book of John in the New Testament of the Christian Bible.

[10] **welded**—bonded; united closely.

I think of it all, I wonder how I can crowd all my joy into one short life. I don't want you to think for one moment that you are bothering me when I write you. It is a real pleasure to do so. You're always so good to let me tell you everything. I am only afraid of trying your patience too far. Even in this long letter I can't tell you all I want to; so I shall write you again soon. Jerrine will write too. Just now she has very sore fingers. She has been picking gooseberries, and they have been pretty severe on her brown little paws.

With much love to you, I am

"Honest and truly" yours,

ELINORE RUPERT STEWART.

QUESTIONS TO CONSIDER

1. How might Elinore Stewart's letter writing have helped her live with her decision to be a homesteader in Wyoming?

2. Why did Elinore Stewart marry so quickly? What apprehensions does she have about her hasty wedding?

3. What does Elinore Stewart fear she and Becky Sharp may have in common? In Stewart's place, what might a more traditional woman have done?

4. Why do you think Elinore Stewart gave up her plans to travel?

5. What is your opinion of Elinore Stewart's statement that she is happy in her marriage to Mr. Stewart?

6. In what ways could Elinore Stewart be considered a rebel?

General Review of the Sex Situation

BY DOROTHY PARKER

Dorothy Parker (1893–1967) was born in New York City. Both her parents had died by the time she was in her late teens, and she got a job writing photo captions for Vogue *magazine. It was at this age that she first began to write poetry that expressed her mixed feelings about love. After being transferred to* Vanity Fair *magazine, Parker became part of the Algonquin Club. This small group of sophisticated New York writers were known for their witty, sarcastic insults and famous "wisecracks," of which Parker's were considered the most bitter of the lot. This poem is from* Enough Rope *(1926).*

Woman wants **monogamy**; [1]
Man delights in **novelty**.[2]
Love is woman's moon and sun;
Man has other forms of fun.

---

[1] **monogamy**—the practice of being married to only one person.
[2] **novelty**—newness; new things.

Woman lives but in her lord;
Count to ten, and man is bored.
With this the **gist**[3] and sum of it,
What earthly good can come of it?

---

[3] **gist**—central idea; essence.

QUESTIONS TO CONSIDER

1. What opposites does Parker present in her poem? Do you think she sides with one sex or the other? Why or why not?

2. What specific word choices exemplify the "wisecracks" for which Parker is famous?

3. In what sense is Parker a rebel? Who or what is she rebelling against?

I Became Interested in Flying

BY AMELIA EARHART

*Famed female aviator Amelia Earhart (1897–1935) became the
first woman to fly solo across the Atlantic Ocean. She flew from
Newfoundland to Ireland on May 20, 1932. In 1937, she vanished
on an attempted flight around the world. No traces of her plane
or her body were ever found. In this excerpt from her book* The
Fun of It: Random Records of My Own Flying and of Women
in Aviation *(1932), Earhart recalls her early fascination with
flying and talks about how she turned her dream of becoming
a professional aviator into a reality.*

After graduation from High School (where I had
become greatly interested in chemistry and physics)
I waited around a year and then entered Ogontz
School, near Philadelphia. During Christmas vacation
of my senior year I went to Toronto, where my sister
was entered at St. Margaret's College. There for the

first time I realized what the World War[1] meant. Instead of new uniforms and brass bands, I saw only the results of a four years' desperate struggle; men without arms and legs, men who were paralyzed and men who were blind.

One day I saw four one-legged men at once, walking as best they could down the street together.

"Mother, I'd like to stay here and help in the hospitals," I said when I returned home. "I can't bear the thought of going back to school and being so useless."

"That means giving up graduating," said Mother.

I didn't care. I gave up all thought of returning to school and took steps to become a nurse's aide. Though I endeavored to connect with the American Red Cross, somehow the papers were never completed and I spent months in Toronto working in a hospital until the Armistice.[2]

Nurse's aides did everything from scrubbing floors to playing tennis with **convalescing**[3] patients. The patients called us "sister" and we hotfooted here and there to attend their wants.

"Please rub my back, sister. I'm so tired lying in bed." Or, "Won't you bring me ice cream today instead of rice pudding?"

We were on duty from seven in the morning until seven at night with two hours off in the afternoon. I spent a great deal of time in the diet kitchen and later in the dispensary[4]—because I knew a little chemistry. Probably the fact that I could be trusted not to drink up the medical supply of whisky counted more than the chemistry.

---

[1] World War—World War I, fought among the major European powers and their allies on the continents of Europe, Africa, and Asia from 1914–1918.

[2] Armistice—truce that ended World War I. It was signed on November 11, 1918.

[3] **convalescing**—slowly recovering.

[4] dispensary—place where medicines and prescriptions are prepared and given out.

When the influenza epidemic struck town, I was one of the few volunteers permitted to be on night duty. I was transferred to a pneumonia ward and helped to ladle out[5] medicine from buckets in the overcrowded wards of the institution.

I believe it was during the winter of 1918 that I became interested in airplanes. Though I had seen one or two at county fairs before, I now saw many of them, as the officers were trained at the various fields around the city. Of course, no civilian had the opportunity of going up. But I hung around in my spare time and absorbed all I could. I remember the sting of the snow on my face as it was blown back from the propellers when the training planes took off on skis.

Time rolled on and I was still in Toronto at the time of the Armistice. What a day!

All day long whistles kept up a continuous blowing. No means of transportation was available and every one had to walk downtown, and did so I think. Private cars ran the risk of being stalled in the littered streets and the traction company[6] just gave up and let its trolleys stand. Young men ran around with huge dusters of flour and blew it on young women.

"Hey girlie, the war's over!" Plop! And the victim looked like a snow man. Supposedly dignified citizens snake-danced and knocked each other's hats off. I didn't hear a serious word of thanksgiving in all the hullaballoo!

At the end of my brief hospital career, I became a patient myself. It was probably the case of trying to carry on all day as usual and work all night. Anyway, I collected a bug which took up residence in the inaccessible little hole behind one's cheek called the antrum. The result was several minor operations and a rather long

---

[5] ladle out—dispense with a deep-bowled, long-handled spoon.

[6] traction company—business responsible for moving stalled trolley cars.

period of convalescence. Some of this was spent at Northampton[7] where my sister was at Smith College and the rest at Lake George.[8] While in "Hamp," I took a course in automobile engine repair, which laid the foundation of any practical knowledge of motors I have gained since.

But I had acquired a **yen**[9] for medicine, and I planned to fit myself for such a career. Consequently I went to New York and entered Columbia University. There I took what I could of all the University "ologies"[10] which should help toward that calling, mixed with a luxury course in French literature. As usual I had a good time, though I studied hard and didn't have much money. But students in New York can get so much with so little if they really wish. The steps in the gallery of Carnegie Hall are really not uncomfortable and I enjoyed many a concert from that locality—after I got used to the smell of garlic. Even the Palisades across the river were good for hiking and the cost to get there by ferry is only a few cents.

I suppose I must have been fairly stalwart-looking[11] for on one of the periodic jaunts to the Palisades, the shopkeeper in a little store where three other hikers and I had stopped to buy sandwiches for lunch, eyed our small group and said,

"I bet you girls iss yust off the farm."

It just happened that none of us had ever been on a farm at that time, but the man behind the counter was probably not used to city people's spending their holidays as we were doing.

---

[7] Northampton—town in Massachusetts.

[8] Lake George—a town located in upstate New York.

[9] **yen**—strong desire or longing.

[10] "ologies"—refers to classes ending in "ology," such as biology, physiology, psychology, and so forth.

[11] stalwart-looking—physically strong-looking.

I was familiar with all the forbidden underground passageways which connected the different buildings of the University. I think I explored every nook and cranny possible. I have sat in the lap of the gilded statue which decorates the library steps, and I was probably the most frequent visitor on the top of the library dome. I mean the top.

I used my knowledge of how to get on the dome a few years later when I was again at Columbia. It proved an excellent vantage point for watching the eclipse of the sun in 1925. I stood there with a well-known biologist and looked across at the angel trumpeting on the highest point of St. John's Cathedral. We three appeared to have a better view of the galloping moon shadows than anyone else in the world.

The only other eclipse of the sun I have seen was from the air. I was caught between the mainland and Catalina in the weird darkness of the **phenomenon**[12] in 1924.

My knowledge of the passageways at Columbia has not yet proved useful, but that could be said of other things one learns at college, too.

It took me only a few months to discover that I probably should not make the ideal physician. Though I liked learning all about medicine, particularly the experimental side, visions of its practical application floored me. For instance, I thought among other possibilities of sitting at the bedside of a hypochondriac[13] and handing out **innocuous**[14] sugar-pellets to a patient with an imaginary illness.

"If you'll take these pills," I heard myself saying in a professional tone, "the pain in your knee will be much less, if not entirely eliminated."

This picture made me feel inadequate and insincere. I did not see then that there was just as much

---

[12] **phenomenon**—unusual occurrence.

[13] hypochondriac—person who has a persistent belief that one is or is about to become ill.

[14] **innocuous**—harmless.

of a problem in curing the somewhat mentally ill as those physically so—even though the methods used might differ.

But when you are young, you are apt to make important decisions for reasons that later on seem quite **superficial**.[15] And I decided against medicine in just this way, **hearkening**[16] to the pleadings of my mother and father, leaving Columbia and going to California.

When I left New York I intended to follow up Medical Research—that, at least, still greatly appealed to me in the field of medicine. But somehow, I did not get into the swing of the western universities before aviation caught me. The interest aroused in me in Toronto led me to all the air circuses in the vicinity. And, by dragging my father around and prompting him to inquiries, I became more and more interested.

One day he and I were among the spectators at a meet at Long Beach.

"Dad, please ask that officer how long it takes to fly," I said, pointing out a doggy[17] young man in uniform.

"Apparently it differs with different people," my good parent reported after some investigation, "though the average seems to be from five to ten hours."

"Please find out how much lessons cost," I continued.

"The answer to that is a thousand dollars. But why do you want to know?"

I wasn't really sure. Anyway, such were second-hand conversations I had with the patient pilots of those days. And, somehow or other, I felt in my bones that a hop[18] would come soon.

The field where I first went up is a residential suburb of Los Angeles. Then it was simply an open space on

---

[15] **superficial**—shallow.

[16] **hearkening**—paying close attention.

[17] doggy—stylish.

[18] hop—ride.

Wilshire Boulevard, surrounded by oil wells. The pilot of the airplane has since become famous as one of the greatest **exponents**[19] of speed in the world. His name is Frank Hawks and he holds more records for fast flying than anyone else.

As soon as we left the ground, I knew I myself had to fly. Miles away I saw the ocean and the Hollywood hills seemed to peep over the edge of the cockpit, as if they were already friends.

"I think I'd like to learn to fly," I told the family casually that evening, knowing full well I'd die if I didn't.

"Not a bad idea," said my father just as casually. "When do you start?" It would need some investigation I told him, but I'd let him know shortly. Mother seemed equally non-combative.

There were no regular schools at the time, and instruction was mostly given by men who had returned from the war. Within a few days I had signed up for lessons, and went home with the proposition that somebody pay for them.

"You really weren't serious, were you?" my father said in surprise. "I thought you were just wishing. I can't afford to let you have instruction."

I saw if he had ever liked the idea, he was completely unsold then. Evidently, he thought that if he didn't pay, I would not fly. But I was determined and got my first job—in the telephone company, it was—to pay for the lessons I so dearly wanted.

From then on the family scarcely saw me for I worked all the week and spent what I had of Saturday and Sunday at the airport a few miles from town. The trip there took more than an hour to the end of the carline,[20] and then a walk of several miles along the dusty highway. In those days it was really necessary for

---

[19] **exponents**—symbols.

[20] carline—public transportation system.

a woman to wear breeks[21] and a leather coat. The fields were dusty and hard to climb into. Flyers dressed the part in semi-military outfits and in order to be as inconspicuous as possible, I fell into the same style.

One day as I was striding along the dusty road, a friendly motorist offered me a lift. My costume and destination explained my errand. There was a little girl in the car who became exceedingly excited when she found out for a certainty that I flew.

"But you don't look like an aviatrix.[22] You have long hair."

Up to that time I had been snipping inches off my hair secretly, but I had not bobbed[23] it lest people think me **eccentric**.[24] For in 1920 it was very odd indeed for a woman to fly, and I had tried to remain as normal as possible in looks in order to offset the usual criticism of my behavior.

My learning to fly was rather a long-drawn-out process, principally because—no pay, no fly and no work, no pay. However, when the time at last came to **solo**,[25] the period of training seemed to act to banish nervousness. I went up five thousand feet and played around a little and came back.

"How did it feel?" the watchers on the ground wanted to know when I returned. "Were you scared?"

"I sang," confessed one pilot who was standing nearby, "as loud as I could."

I felt silly. I hadn't done anything special. My first solo had come and gone without anything to mark it but an exceptionally poor landing.

---

[21] breeks—men's trousers that extend just below the knee.

[22] aviatrix—female pilot.

[23] bobbed—cut short.

[24] **eccentric**—different or deviating from the norm.

[25] **solo**—fly alone without a teacher.

"You didn't do anything right but land rottenly," said another pilot. "Don't you know you're supposed to be so ground shy you stay up until the gas tank runs dry?"

After I had really flown alone, Mother was good sport enough to help me buy a small second hand plane. It happened to be the only one the builder had so he and I worked out a scheme to use it jointly. For free hangar[26] space to me, he was privileged to demonstrate with it. As both of us were equally fond of the little contraption and equally **impecunious**,[27] this arrangement worked very well. And I spent many hours in this and other planes I occasionally had a chance to fly.

If Mother was worried during this period, she did not show it. Possibly, except for backing me financially, she could have done nothing more helpful. I didn't realize it at the time, but the cooperation of one's family and close friends is one of the greatest safety factors a **fledgling**[28] flyer can have.

After a year had passed, I achieved the only type of license issued at that time, the *Federation Aeronautique Internationale*. And Mother was so interested by this time I am sure she would have accepted a ride with me. However, I did not start her aeronautical education until a long while afterward.

In passing I should call attention to the fact that it wasn't really necessary to have any license at this period. There were no regulations such as exist today. People just flew, when and if they could, in anything which would get off the ground. Methods of teaching flying have greatly improved over those of the dim dark ages when I learned. There were no schools then, as we

---

[26] hangar—covered space for parking and repairing an airplane.

[27] **impecunious**—lacking money or wealth.

[28] **fledgling**—new and inexperienced.

know them now, nor standardized equipment. Fundamentally, of course, the principles are just the same and so are the fledgling flyers.

Perhaps the easiest way for me to give a picture of what flying instruction is like is to tell just what I had to do at first, and, to compare that with the present[29] requirements for obtaining a flyer's license. As I have said, my training took place in California. The plane used was a Curtiss Canuck very like the famous Jenny of war time memory. Both of these planes and their motors, as well, have been replaced by improved equipment.

In 1920, two years after the Armistice, airplanes were not so well built as at present and motors had habits of stopping at **inopportune**[30] moments. Pilots just naturally expected to have to **sit down**[31] every so often because of engine failure. The power plants[32] of today are a happy contrast. It is rare indeed that one "conks,"[33] if properly cared for, so great has been the increase in reliability. Consequently, the modern pilot's attitude is quite different from that of the post-war flier.

The development of flying is somehow synonymous with automobiling of a decade ago. If you don't remember, your parents will, the Sunday rides of yesterday. Roadsides were always lined with cars in trouble—some with flat tires, and some with puzzled, begoggled drivers peering under raised hoods at engines they didn't understand. To add to the complications, there were few service stations and few good roads.

Now, yours may be among the 20,000 cars going to a football game, say, not one of which will experience a single mechanical failure on the way.

---

[29] present—refers to 1932.

[30] **inopportune**—inconvenient.

[31] **sit down**—land suddenly.

[32] power plants—a reference to the more powerful, dependable planes of the early 1930s.

[33] conks—stops working.

QUESTIONS TO CONSIDER

1. In what ways does Amelia Earhart push the boundaries of acceptance and appropriate behavior for women of her time?

2. What tactics does she use to offset possible criticism of her actions?

3. Who are Earhart's allies in her decision to fly? Why are allies important to anyone wishing to go against family or societal expectations?

4. What is Earhart's general attitude toward her life? What helps her achieve perspective on her life?

5. What aspects of Earhart's character do you think might have contributed to the American public's excitement over her achievements and its mourning when she was lost?

Karate

BY DOROTHY ALLISON

Born in South Carolina in 1949, Dorothy Allison writes poetry, fiction, and essays that reflect her interest in the plight of poor southern women. She was born into poverty and overcame great obstacles to break out of a family cycle of ignorance and abuse. The first member of her family to finish high school, she won a National Merit Scholarship and went on to complete college and graduate school. She has been writing most of her life, but until she was twenty-four, she burned everything she ever wrote. Then friends persuaded her that her writing had value, and she began to keep it. Today, she is an award-winning author of six books. Her memoir, Two or Three Things I Know for Sure *(1955), from which the following excerpt comes, began as a performance piece. In it she explores love and loss, beauty and terror, and family love and hatred. Here, Allison describes the passion for learning karate that gave her comfort during an awkward adolescence.*

At twenty-four I joined a karate class and learned for the first time how to run without fear pushing me. It was not what I had intended. I never expected to join the class at all. I showed up because I had been told there were no women allowed and my newfound feminist convictions insisted someone had to do something about that. Along with my friend Flo, I dressed in loose clothes and hitched a ride out to the university gardens very early one Monday morning.

On a rutted dirt road lane a small group of **peevish-looking**[1] young males were climbing out of rusty old cars and pulling off shoes.

"Where's the sensei?"[2] I demanded of one of those boys. He stared at me blankly. I stared right back and repeated my question.

That boy just stood there, looking from me to Flo to his friends. Then somebody laughed. Flo and I glared fiercely. One of the boys stepped forward and gave me a nod.

"Down there," he said. "A quarter mile down that path. The class is out there where the teacher's waiting." Then he nodded again and took off in an easy **lope**.[3] The other boys stepped around us and followed.

I watched their bare feet pick up fine dust and kick it into the cool, moist grass along the path. Without thought, Flo and I fell in behind them. It was a long, winding run down into a hollow and then up around a wide grassy hill. My thighs and calves started to ache in the first thirty feet. Only stubbornness kept me moving, following those boys, who would occasionally look back and snicker. Later I would be grateful for their laughter. Without it, I would never have managed the full quarter mile, especially not the last curving uphill grade to where a soft-featured, blond young man was doing some kind of stylized kicking exercise.

The sensei stopped to watch us stagger up the hill. The boys were ahead of us, and I couldn't hear what they told him, but his first words were as precise as his motions.

---

[1] **peevish-looking**—appearing ill-tempered or irritable.

[2] sensei—karate teacher.

[3] **lope**—long, bounding step.

"You want to join the class, you'll have to do better than that."

"We will," I announced **emphatically**,[4] trying not to gasp for air. The sensei just nodded and started the class, putting Flo and me at the back as if suddenly adding two women to his all-male domain were something he had hoped to do all along—which it was, though we knew nothing of that.

The first weeks we kept coming just to hear the sensei tell us we could not come back. But every day he welcomed us as he welcomed the boys, requiring that we first complete that run, then stand silent, breathing as he breathed, deep and slow, trying to feel each muscle in hips and shoulders and neck. I barely heard him. For me those weeks were grim agony. I was making demands on muscles I had ignored most of my life, and only because I expected the ordeal to be over soon.

The boys helped. Every time they laughed, I would make myself stand taller or move faster. Every time they looked back over their shoulders at my stumbling attempts at running, I would grit my teeth and force my legs to pump higher. So long as they laughed, I would not quit. So long as they watched for tears, I would not let myself cry, though some days to cry was what I wanted most to do—to lie down in the damp grass and weep at the **inept**[5] female body in which I was imprisoned.

Two, three, four weeks, we kept going. The laughter eased off, but not my desire to cry. Was it in the fourth week or the fifth that the teacher brought his wife to class? A ballet dancer with long, long legs, she easily out-distanced all of us on tight-muscled calves. Nothing **daunted**[6] that woman, not the run or the kicking or even

---

[4] **emphatically**—enthusiastically, with determination.

[5] **inept**—clumsy, useless.

[6] **daunted**—deterred or discouraged.

lifting one of those big pink-faced boys to her shoulders and showing us how to step in a gracefully wide stance while holding him easily. I watched her in confusion, understanding completely what was intended, the example of that astonishingly perfected female body taking over the class and showing us all what a woman could do. I watched the sensei watching her and understood that not only would he not ask us to leave his class but that the passion in his glance was something rare and unknown to me: love that yearned as much for the spirit as for the body.

I looked at her then as he looked at her, and somehow she became a story in my head, a memory of a woman I had seen once dancing on the balls of her feet, arms moving like scythes,[7] face stern, eyes alive. Naked and powerful, deadly and utterly at peace with herself. She had a body that had never forgotten itself, and I knew at once that what I was seeing was magic. Watching, I fell in love—not with her but with the body itself, the hope of movement, the power of jumping and thrusting and being the creature that is not afraid to fall down but somehow doesn't anyway.

Running the quarter mile back from that class, I started to cry. I made no sound, no gesture, just kept moving and letting the teardrops sheet down my face. Everyone was way ahead of me. My hands were curled into fists, pumping at my sides. The tears became sobs, heartbroken and angry, and I stumbled, almost falling down before I caught my footing in a different gait. My hips shifted. Something in the bottom of my spine let go. Something disconnected from the coccyx[8] that was shattered when I was a girl. Something loosened from the old bruised and torn flesh. Some piece of shame pulled free, some shame so ancient I had never known myself without it. I felt it

---

[7] scythes—farm tools with long curved handles.

[8] coccyx—tailbone.

lift, and with it my thighs lifted, suddenly loose and strong, pumping steadily beneath me as if nothing could hold me down.

I picked up speed and closed in on the boys ahead of me, Flo there among them like a female gazelle.[9] I saw her head turn and discover me running just behind her. She ignored my wet face and produced a welcoming grin, then stepped aside so that we were running together, elbow to elbow, her legs setting a pace for mine. I breathed deep and felt the muscles in my neck open, something strong getting stronger. If there was love in the world, I thought, then there was no reason I should not have it in my life. I matched Flo's pace and kept running.

I fell in love with karate though I remained a white belt,[10] year after year of white belts—a legendary white belt, in fact. I was so bad, people would come to watch. Inflexible, nearsighted, without talent or aptitude, falling down, sweaty and miserable—sometimes I would even pass out halfway through the class. I learned to take a glass of bouillon[11] like medicine before I put on my gi.[12] But I kept going back, careless of injury or laughter. What I wanted from karate was some echo of love for my body and the spirit it houses—meat and bone and the liquid song of my own gasps, the liquor stink of stubborn sweat, the sweet burn of sinew,[13] muscle, and lust.

I studied karate for eight years, going from school to school, city to city, always starting over. My first sensei was the best I ever found. That moment of perfect physical consciousness was more often memory than reality. I did not become suddenly coordinated,

---

[9] gazelle—small, graceful, and swift African and Asian antelope.

[10] white belt—the first level of mastery in karate.

[11] bouillon—a clear, seasoned soup.

[12] gi—karate belt.

[13] sinew—tendon or nerve. In this case it refers to solid strength or power.

develop perfect vision in my near-blind right eye, or turn jock and take up half a dozen sports. All I gained was a sense of what I might do, could do if I worked at it, a sense of my body as my own. And that was miracle enough.

QUESTIONS TO CONSIDER

1. What are Allison's initial reasons for wanting to learn karate? How physically prepared is she to learn this new discipline? How mentally and emotionally ready is she? What does she end up learning, and why is it such a surprise to her?

2. How do adversity and the reactions of the boys in particular spur her on?

3. In what ways would you consider Allison to be a rebel?

4. Why is the ballet dancer such a strong role model for Allison?

5. Who or what is Allison running from in the beginning? As time goes on, who or what is she running toward? In the process what does she let go of?

The Water Faucet Vision

BY GISH JEN

*Chinese-American writer Gish Jen (1955–   ) changed her name
from Lillian to Gish, after the star of silent films, in high school.
She has written two novels,* Typical American *and* Mona in the
Promised Land. *The following story is from* Who's Irish?, *a collection
of Jen's short stories that won the 1999 National Book Critics Circle
Award. In it, Jen writes with honesty about the challenges facing
immigrant families, including her own. In this story, she addresses the
awkwardness of communication between two generations of Chinese
immigrants and the narrator's attempts to understand the truth about
herself, her family, and the nature of faith.*

To protect my sister Mona and me from the pains—
or, as they pronounced it, the "pins"—of life, my parents
did their fighting in Shanghai[1] dialect, which we didn't
understand; and when my father one day pitched a

---

[1] Shanghai—largest city in China.

brass vase through the kitchen window, my mother told us he had done it by accident.

"By accident?" said Mona.

My mother chopped the foot off a mushroom.

"By accident?" said Mona. "By *accident?*"

Later I tried to explain to her that she shouldn't have persisted like that, but it was hopeless.

"What's the matter with throwing things," she shrugged. "He was *mad.*"

That was the difference between Mona and me: Fighting was just fighting to her. If she worried about anything, it was only that she might turn out too short to become a ballerina, in which case she was going to be a piano player.

I, on the other hand, was going to be a **martyr**.[2] I was in fifth grade then, and the hyperimaginative sort—the kind of girl who grows **morbid**[3] in Catholic school, who longs to be chopped or frozen to death but then has nightmares about it from which she wakes up screaming and clutching a stuffed bear. It was not a bear that I clutched, though, but a string of three malachite[4] beads that I had found in the marsh by the old aqueduct[5] one day. Apparently once part of a necklace, they were each wonderfully **striated**[6] and swirled, and slightly humped toward the center, like a jellyfish; so that if I squeezed one, it would slip smoothly away, with a grace that altogether enthralled and—on those dream-harrowed nights—soothed me, soothed me as nothing had before or has since. Not that I've lacked occasion for soothing: Though it's been four months since my mother died, there are still nights when sleep stands away from me, stiff as a well-paid sentry. But

---

[2] **martyr**—someone who suffers death rather than deny a religious faith.

[3] **morbid**—focused on death.

[4] malachite—made from a green semi-precious stone.

[5] aqueduct—pipe or channel for carrying large amounts of moving water.

[6] **striated**—banded or streaked with stripes.

that is another story. Back then I had my malachite beads, and if I worried[7] them long and patiently enough, I was sure to start feeling better, more awake, even a little special—imagining, as I liked to, that my nightmares were communications from the Almighty Himself, preparation for my painful destiny. Discussing them with Patty Creamer, who had also promised her life to God, I called them "almost visions"; and Patty, her mouth wadded with the three or four sticks of doublemint she always seemed to have going at once, said, "I bet you'll be doin' miracleth by seventh grade."

Miracles. Today Patty laughs to think she ever spent good time stewing on such matters, her attention having long turned to rugs, and artwork, and antique Japanese bureaus—things she believes in.

"A good bureau's more than just a bureau," she explained last time we had lunch. "It's a hedge[8] against life. I tell you, if there's one thing I believe, it's that cheap stuff's just money out the window. Nice stuff, on the other hand—now *that* you can always cash out, if life gets rough. *That* you can count on."

In fifth grade, though, she counted on different things.

"You'll be doing miracles too," I told her, but she shook her shaggy head and looked doleful.

"Na' me," she chomped. "Buzzit's okay. The kin' things I like, prayers work okay on."

"Like?"

"Like you 'member that dreth I liked?"

She meant the yellow one, with the criss-cross straps.

"Well gueth what."

"Your mom got it for you."

She smiled. "And I only jutht prayed for it for a week," she said.

---

[7] worried—touched repeatedly.

[8] hedge—protection.

As for myself, though, I definitely wanted to be able to perform a wonder or two. Miracle-working! It was the carrot of carrots:[9] It kept me doing my homework, taking the sacraments;[10] it kept me mournfully on key in music hour, while my classmates hiccuped and squealed their carefree hearts away. Yet I couldn't have said what I wanted such powers *for*, exactly. That is, I thought of them the way one might think of, say, an ornamental sword—as a kind of collectible, which also happened to be a means of defense.

But then Patty's father walked out on her mother, and for the first time, there was a miracle I wanted to do. I wanted it so much I could see it: Mr. Creamer made into a spitball; Mr. Creamer shot through a straw into the sky; Mr. Creamer unrolled and re-plumped, plop back on Patty's doorstep. I would've cleaned out his mind and given him a shave **en route**.[11] I would've given him a box of peanut fudge, tied up with a ribbon, to present to Patty with a kiss.

But instead all I could do was try to tell her he'd come back.

"He will not, he will not!" she sobbed. "He went on a boat to Rio Deniro.[12] To Rio Deniro!"

I tried to offer her a stick of gum, but she wouldn't take it.

"He said he would rather look at water than at my mom's fat face. He said he would rather look at water than at me." Now she was really wailing, and holding her ribs so tightly that she almost seemed to be hurting herself—so tightly that just looking at her arms wound around her like snakes made my heart feel squeezed.

---

[9] carrot of carrots—supreme motivation, from the fable about a man who makes a donkey move by hanging a carrot in front of its nose.

[10] sacraments—formal religious acts.

[11] **en route**—on the way, in French.

[12] Rio Deniro—Patty has confused the Brazilian city Rio de Janeiro with the movie actor Robert De Niro.

I patted her on the arm. A one-winged pigeon waddled by.

"He said I wasn't even his kid, he said I came from Uncle Johnny. He said I was garbage, just like my mom and Uncle Johnny. He said I wasn't even his kid, he said I wasn't his Patty, he said I came from Uncle Johnny!"

"From your Uncle Johnny?" I said stupidly.

"From Uncle Johnny," she cried. "From Uncle Johnny!"

"He said that?" I said. Then, wanting to go on, to say *something,* I said, "Oh Patty, don't cry."

She kept crying.

I tried again. "Oh Patty, don't cry," I said. Then I said, "Your dad was a jerk anyway."

The pigeon produced a large runny dropping.

It was a good twenty minutes before Patty was calm enough for me just to run to the girls' room to get her some toilet paper; and by the time I came back she was sobbing again, saying "To Rio Deniro, to Rio Deniro" over and over again, as though the words had stuck in her and couldn't be gotten out. As we had missed the regular bus home and the late bus too, I had to leave her a second time to go call my mother, who was only mad until she heard what had happened. Then she came and picked us up, and bought us each a Fudgsicle.

Some days later, Patty and I started a program to work on getting her father home. It was a serious business. We said extra prayers, and lit votive candles;[13] I tied my malachite beads to my uniform belt, fondling them as though they were a rosary, I a nun. We even took to walking about the school halls with our hands folded—a sight so **ludicrous**[14] that our wheeze of a principal personally took us aside one day.

---

[13] votive candles—small candles in some Catholic churches that people light when they offer personal prayers.

[14] **ludicrous**—absurd, amusing.

"I must tell you," she said, using her nose as a speaking tube, "that there is really no need for such peee-ity."[15]

But we persisted, promising to marry God and praying to every saint we could think of. We gave up gum, then gum and slim jims both, then gum and slim jims and ice cream—and when even that didn't work, we started on more innovative things. The first was looking at flowers. We held our hands beside our eyes like blinders as we hurried by the violets by the flagpole, the window box full of tulips outside the nurse's office. Next it was looking at boys: Patty gave up angel-eyed Jamie Halloran and I, gymnastic Anthony Rossi. It was hard, but in the end our efforts paid off. Mr. Creamer came back a month later, and though he brought with him nothing but **dysentery**,[16] he was at least too sick to have all that much to say.

Then, in the course of a fight with my father, my mother somehow fell out of their bedroom window.

Recently—thinking a mountain vacation might cheer me—I sublet my apartment to a handsome but somber newlywed couple, who turned out to be every bit as responsible as I'd hoped. They cleaned out even the eggshell chips I'd sprinkled around the base of my plants as fertilizer, leaving behind only a shiny silver-plate cake server and a list of their hopes and goals for the summer. The list, tacked **precariously**[17] to the back of the kitchen door, began with a **fervent**[18] appeal to God to help them get their wedding thank-yous written in three weeks or less. (You could see they had originally written "two weeks" but scratched it out—no miracles being demanded here.) It went on:

---

[15] peee-ity—piety, or religious devotion.

[16] **dysentery**—a disease characterized by severe diarrhea.

[17] **precariously**—in the way of danger.

[18] **fervent**—deeply felt.

Please help us, Almighty Father in Heaven Above, to get Ann a teaching job within a half-hour drive of here in a nice neighborhood.

Please help us, Almighty Father in Heaven Above, to get John a job doing anything where he won't strain his back and that is within a half-hour drive of here.

Please help us, Almighty Father in Heaven Above, to get us a car.

Please help us, A.F. in H.A., to learn French.

Please help us, A.F. in H.A., to find seven dinner recipes that cost less than 60 cents a serving and can be made in a half-hour. And that don't have tomatoes, since You in Your Heavenly Wisdom made John allergic.

Please help us, A.F. in H.A., to avoid books in this apartment such as You in Your Heavenly Wisdom allowed John, for Your Heavenly Reasons, to find three nights ago (June 2nd).

Et cetera. In the left-hand margin they kept score of how they had fared with their requests, and it was heartening to see that nearly all of them were marked "Yes! Praise the Lord!" (sometimes shortened to PTL), with the sole exception of learning French, which was mysteriously marked "No! PTL to the Highest."

That note touched me. Strange and familiar both, it seemed like it had been written by some cousin of mine—some cousin who had stayed home to grow up, say, while I went abroad and learned what I had to, though the learning was painful. This, of course, is just a manner of speaking; in fact, I did my growing up at home, like anybody else.

But the learning *was* painful: I never knew exactly how it happened that my mother went hurtling through the air that night years ago, only that the wind had been chopping at the house, and that the argument had started about the state of the roof. Someone had been up to fix it the year before, but it wasn't a roofer, it was some man my father had insisted could do just as good a job for a quarter of the price. And maybe he could have, had he not somehow managed to step through a knot in the wood under the shingles and break his uninsured ankle. Now the shingles were coming loose again, and the attic insulation was mildewing[19] besides, and my father was wanting to sell the house altogether, which he said my mother had wanted to buy so she could send pictures of it home to her family in China.

"The Americans have a saying," he said. "They saying, 'You have to keep up with the Jones family.' I'm saying if the Jones family in Shanghai, you can send any picture you want, *an-y* picture. Go take picture of those rich guys' house. You want to act like rich guys, right? Go take picture of those rich guys' house."

At that point my mother sent Mona and me to wash up, and started speaking Shanghaiese. They argued for some time in the kitchen, while we listened from the top of the stairs, our faces wedged between the bumpy Spanish scrolls of the wrought iron railing. First my mother ranted, then my father, then they both ranted at once until finally there was a thump, followed by a long quiet.

"Do you think they're kissing now?" said Mona. "I bet they're kissing, like this." She pursed her lips like a fish and was about to put them to the railing when we heard my mother locking the back door. We hightailed it into bed; my parents creaked up the stairs. Everything at that point seemed fine. Once in their bedroom, though, they started up again, first softly, then louder and louder, until my mother turned on a radio to try to disguise the noise. A door slammed; they began shouting at one another; another door slammed; a shoe or something banged the wall behind Mona's bed.

---

[19] mildewing—becoming infected with a white fungi growth.

"How're we supposed to *sleep?*" said Mona, sitting up.

There was another thud, more yelling in Shanghaiese, and then my mother's voice pierced the wall, in English. "So what you want I should do? Go to work like Theresa Lee?"

My father rumbled something back.

"You think you're big shot because you have job, right? You're big shot, but you never get promotion, you never get raise. All I do is spend money, right? So what do you do, you tell me. So what do you do!"

Something hit the floor so hard that our room shook.

"So kill me," screamed my mother. "You know what you are? You are failure. Failure! You are failure!"

Then there was a sudden, terrific, bursting crash—and after it, as if on a bungled cue, the serene blare of an a cappella[20] soprano, picking her way down a scale.

By the time Mona and I knew to look out the window, a neighbor's pet beagle was already on the scene, sniffing and barking at my mother's body, his tail crazy with excitement; then he was barking at my stunned and trembling father, at the shrieking ambulance, the police, at crying Mona in her bunny-footed pajamas, and at me, barefoot in the cold grass, squeezing her shoulder with one hand and clutching my malachite beads with the other.

My mother wasn't dead, only unconscious, the paramedics figured that out right away, but there was blood everywhere, and though they were reassuring about her head wounds as they strapped her to the stretcher, commenting also on how small she was, how delicate, how light, my father kept saying, "I killed her, I killed her" as the ambulance screeched and screeched headlong, forever, to the hospital. I was afraid to touch her, and glad of the metal rail between us, even though its sturdiness made her seem even frailer than she was;

---

[20] a cappella—without accompaniment, a musical term from Italian.

I wished she was bigger, somehow, and noticed, with a pang, that the new red slippers we had given her for Mother's Day had been lost somewhere along the way. How much she seemed to be leaving behind, as we careened along[21]—still not there, still not there—Mona and Dad and the medic and I taking up the whole ambulance, all the room, so there was no room for anything else; no room even for my mother's real self, the one who should have been pinching the color back to my father's gray face, the one who should have been calming Mona's cowlick[22]—the one who should have been bending over us, to help us to be strong, to help us get through, even as we bent over her.

Then suddenly we were there, the glowing square of the emergency room entrance opening like the gates of heaven; and immediately the talk of miracles began. Alive, a miracle. No bones broken, a miracle. A miracle that the **hemlocks**[23] cushioned her fall, a miracle that they hadn't been trimmed in a year and a half. It was a miracle that all that blood, the blood that had seemed that night to be everywhere, was from one **shard**[24] of glass, a single shard, can you imagine, and as for the gash in her head, the scar would be covered by hair. The next day my mother cheerfully described just how she would part it so that nothing would show at all.

"You're a lucky duck-duck," agreed Mona, helping herself, with a little *pirouette*,[25] to the cherry atop my mother's chocolate pudding.

That wasn't enough for me, though. I was relieved, yes, but what I wanted by then was a real miracle, not

---

[21] careened along—swayed from side to side.

[22] cowlick—a section of hair that grows in a different direction from other parts, often with a tendency to stick up.

[23] **hemlocks**—evergreen trees.

[24] **shard**—small piece.

[25] *pirouette*—dance movement in which one twirls on one's toes, from French for "spinning top."

for her simply to have survived but for the whole thing never to have happened—for my mother's head never to had to been shaved and bandaged like that, for her high, proud forehead to never have been swollen down over her eyes, for her face and neck and hands never to have been painted so many shades of blue-black, and violet, and chartreuse.[26] I still want those things—for my parents not to have had to live with this affair like a prickle-bush between them, for my father to have been able to look my mother in her swollen eyes and curse the madman, the monster that could have dared done this to the woman he loved. I wanted to be able to touch my mother without shuddering, to be able to console my father, to be able to get that crash out of my head, the sound of that soprano—so many things that I didn't know how to pray for them, that I wouldn't have known where to start even if I had the power to work miracles, right there, right then.

A week later, when my mother was home, and her head beginning to bristle with new hairs, I lost my malachite beads. I had been carrying them in a white cloth pouch that Patty had given me, and was swinging the pouch on my pinky on my way home from school, when I swung just a bit too hard, and it went sailing in a long arc through the air, whooshing like a perfectly thrown basketball through one of those holes of a nearby sewer. There was no chance of fishing it out: I looked and looked, crouching on the sticky pavement until the asphalt had crazed the skin of my hands and knees, but all I could discern was an evil-smelling musk, glassy and smug and impenetrable.

My loss didn't quite hit me until I was home, but then it produced an agony all out of proportion to my

---

[26] chartreuse—a brilliant yellow green.

string of pretty beads. I hadn't cried at all during my mother's accident, and now I was crying all afternoon, all through dinner, and then after dinner too, crying past the point where I knew what I was crying for, wishing dimly that I had my beads to hold, wishing dimly that I could pray but refusing, refusing, I didn't know why, until I finally fell into an exhausted sleep on the couch, where my parents left me for the night— glad, no doubt, that one of the more tedious of my childhood crises seemed to be finally winding off the reel of life, onto the reel of memory. They covered me, and somehow grew a pillow under my head, and, with uncharacteristic disregard for the living-room rug, left some milk and pecan sandies on the coffee table, in case I woke up hungry. Their thoughtfulness was **prescient**:[27] I did wake up in the early part of the night; and it was then, amid the unfamiliar sounds and shadows of the living room, that I had what I was sure was a true vision.

Even now what I saw retains an odd clarity: the **requisite**[28] strange light flooding the room, first orange, and then a bright yellow-green, then a crackling bright burst like a Roman candle going off near the piano. There was a distinct smell of coffee, and a long silence. The room seemed to be getting colder. Nothing. A creak; the light starting to wane, then waxing again, brilliant pink now. Still nothing. Then, as the pink started to go a little purple, a perfectly normal middle-aged man's voice, speaking something very like pig latin,[29] told me quietly not to despair, not to despair, my beads would be returned to me.

---

[27] **prescient**—having the characteristic of knowing something before it happens.

[28] **requisite**—essential, necessary.

[29] pig latin—a children's code language in which letters in English words are transposed according to precise rules. "Be right back" is "Ebay ightray ackbay" in pig latin.

That was all. I sat a moment in the dark, then turned on the light, gobbled down the cookies—and in a happy flash understood I was so good, really, so near to being a saint that my malachite beads would come back through the town water system. All I had to do was turn on all the faucets in the house, which I did, one by one, stealing quietly into the bathroom and kitchen and basement. The old spigot[30] by the washing machine was too gunked up to be coaxed very far open, but that didn't matter. The water didn't have to be full blast, I understood that. Then I gathered together my pillow and blanket and trundled up to my bed to sleep.

By the time I woke up in the morning I knew that my beads hadn't shown up, but when I knew it for certain, I was still disappointed; and as if that weren't enough, I had to face my parents and sister, who were all abuzz with the mystery of the faucets. Not knowing what else to do, I, like a puddlebrain, told them the truth. The results were predictably painful.

"Callie had a *vision*," Mona told everyone at the bus stop, "A vision with lights, and sinks in it!"

Sinks, visions. I got it all day, from my parents, from my classmates, even some sixth and seventh graders. Someone drew a cartoon of me with a halo over my head in one of the girls' room stalls; Anthony Rossi made gurgling noises as he walked on his hands at recess. Only Patty tried not to laugh, though even she was something less than **unalloyed**[31] understanding.

"I don't think miracles are thupposed to happen in *thewers*," she said.

Such was the end of my saintly ambitions. It wasn't the end of all holiness; the ideas of purity and goodness

---

[30] spigot—faucet.

[31] **unalloyed**—pure.

still tippled my brain, and over the years I came slowly to grasp of what **grit**[32] true faith was made. Last night, though, when my father called to say that he couldn't go on living in our old house, that he was going to move to a smaller place, another place, maybe a condo—he didn't know how, or where—I found myself still wistful for the time religion seemed all I wanted it to be. Back then the world was a place that could be set right: One had only to direct the hand of the Almighty and say, just here, Lord, we hurt here—and here, and here, and here.

---

[32] **grit**—strength of mind and spirit.

QUESTIONS TO CONSIDER

1. In what ways are Jen and her narrator in this story rebel women? What does Jen's name change have to do with rebellion?

2. How did the narrator's parents try to assimilate into American life and culture and what problems did they face?

3. What did the parents argue about? How did the narrator and Mona see their parents' conflicts? What did the narrator come to understand after her mother's accident?

4. What purpose do the malachite beads serve in the beginning? What in your opinion does the loss of the beads stand for?

5. What does the narrator learn that the newlywed couple seems not to have learned?

6. How would you describe what the narrator learned about "true faith"?

Liberating
Voices

The Solitude of Self

BY ELIZABETH CADY STANTON

Elizabeth Cady Stanton (1815–1902) was a pioneer in the women's suffrage movement. In 1848, she, along with Lucretia Mott, organized the first Woman's Rights Convention at Seneca Falls, New York. With her closest friend Susan B. Anthony, she dedicated her life to gaining voting rights and other rights for women. Although they both died before women gained the right to vote in 1920, their combined voices and courageous work remain one of the most important chapters in American history. The farewell speech Stanton presented as outgoing president of the National American Woman Suffrage Association in 1892, and excerpted here, goes well beyond the issue of suffrage alone. It stands as perhaps the strongest argument ever made for the rights of women.

The strongest reason for giving woman all the opportunities for higher education, for the full development of her **faculties**,[1] her forces of mind and body; for giving her the most enlarged freedom of thought and action; a complete **emancipation**[2] from all forms of bondage, of

---

[1] **faculties**—powers and abilities she was born with.

[2] **emancipation**—freedom.

custom, dependence, superstition; from all the crippling influences of fear—is the solitude and personal responsibility of her own individual life. The strongest reason why we ask for woman a voice in the government under which she lives; in the religion she is asked to believe; equality in social life, where she is the chief factor; a place in the trades and professions, where she may earn her bread, is because of her birthright to self-sovereignty;[3] because, as an individual, she must rely on herself. No matter how much women prefer to lean, to be protected and supported, nor how much men desire to have them do so, they must make the voyage of life alone, and for safety in an emergency, they must know something of the laws of navigation. To guide our own craft, we must be captain, pilot, engineer; with chart and compass to stand at the wheel; to watch the winds and waves, and know when to take in the sail, and to read the signs in the **firmament**[4] over all. It matters not whether the solitary voyager is man or woman; nature, having **endowed**[5] them equally, leaves them to their own skill and judgment in the hour of danger, and, if not equal to the occasion, alike they perish.

To appreciate the importance of fitting every human soul for independent action, think for a moment of the immeasurable solitude of self. We come into the world alone, unlike all who have gone before us, we leave it alone, under circumstances peculiar to ourselves. No mortal ever has been, no mortal ever will be like the soul just launched on the sea of life. There can never again be just such a combination of prenatal[6] influences; never again just such environments as make up the infancy, youth and manhood of this one. . . . Seeing, then, what must be the infinite diversity in human character, we can in a measure appreciate the loss to a nation when any

---

[3] birthright to self-sovereignty—right to govern herself.

[4] **firmament**—sky; heavens.

[5] **endowed**—provided with talents or qualities.

[6] prenatal—referring to those before birth.

large class of the people is uneducated and unrepresented in the government.

. . . The great lesson that nature seems to teach us at all ages is self-dependence, self-protection, self-support. . . .

In youth our most bitter disappointments, our brightest hopes and ambitions, are known only to ourselves. Even our friendship and love we never fully share with another; there is something of every passion, in every situation, we conceal. Even so in our triumphs and our defeats.

We ask no sympathy from others in the anxiety and agony of a broken friendship or shattered love. When death sunders[7] our nearest ties, alone we sit in the shadow of our affliction.[8] Alike amid the greatest triumphs and darkest tragedies of life, we walk alone. On the divine heights of human attainment, eulogized[9] and worshiped as a hero or saint, we stand alone. In ignorance, poverty and vice, as a **pauper**[10] or criminal, alone we starve or steal; alone we suffer the sneers and rebuffs of our fellows; alone we are hunted and hounded through dark courts and alleys, in byways and high-ways; alone we stand in the judgment seat. . . . In hours like these we realize the awful solitude of individual life, its pains, its penalties, its responsibilities. . . .

To throw obstacles in the way of a complete education is like putting out the eyes; to deny the rights of property is like cutting off the hands. To refuse political equality is to rob the ostracized[11] of all self-respect; of credit in the market place; of **recompense**[12] in the world of work, of a voice in choosing those who make and administer the law, a choice in the jury before whom they are tried, and in the judge who decides their punishment.

---

[7] sunders—severs; breaks.

[8] affliction—suffering.

[9] eulogized—praised highly in speeches or writing.

[10] **pauper**—very poor person.

[11] ostracized—ones who are excluded from a group.

[12] **recompense**—payment for a service rendered.

. . .Nothing strengthens the judgment and quickens the conscience like individual responsibility. Nothing adds such dignity to character as the recognition of one's self-sovereignty; the right to an equal place, everywhere conceded—a place earned by personal merit, not an artificial attainment by inheritance, wealth, family and position. Conceding, then, that the responsibilities of life rest equally on man and woman, that their destiny is the same, they need the same preparation for time and eternity. The talk of sheltering woman from the fierce storms of life is the sheerest mockery, for they beat on her from every point of the compass, just as they do on man, and with more fatal results, for he has been trained to protect himself, to resist, and to conquer. Such are the facts in human experience, the responsibilities of individual sovereignty. Rich and poor, intelligent and ignorant, wise and foolish, virtuous and vicious, man and woman; it is ever the same, each soul must depend wholly on itself.

Whatever the theories may be of woman's dependence on man, in the supreme moments of her life, he cannot bear her burdens. Alone she goes to the gates of death, to give life to every man that is born into the world; no one can share her fears, no one can **mitigate**[13] her pangs; and if her sorrow is greater than she can bear, alone she passes beyond the gates into the vast unknown.

. . . But when all artificial trammels[14] are removed, and women are recognized as individuals, responsible for their own environments, thoroughly educated for all positions in life they may be called to fill; with all the resources in themselves that liberal thought and broad culture can give; guided by their own conscience and judgment, trained to self-protection, by a healthy development of the muscular system, and skill in the use of

---

[13] **mitigate**—lessen; alleviate.

[14] trammels—restraints.

weapons and defense; and stimulated to self-support by a knowledge of the business world and the pleasure that **pecuniary**[15] independence must ever give; when women are trained in this way they will in a measure be fitted for those hours of solitude that come alike to all, whether prepared or otherwise.

. . . Whatever may be said of man's protecting power in ordinary conditions, amid all the terrible disasters by land and sea, in the supreme moments of danger, alone woman must ever meet the horrors of the situation.

. . . In that solemn solitude of self, that links us with the immeasurable and the eternal, each soul lives alone forever. A recent writer says: "I remember once, in crossing the Atlantic, to have gone upon the deck of the ship at midnight, when a dense black cloud enveloped the sky, and the great deep was roaring madly under the lashes of demoniac[16] winds. My feeling was not of danger or fear (which is a base[17] surrender of the immortal soul) but of utter desolation and loneliness; a little speck of life shut in by a tremendous darkness. . . ."

And yet, there is a solitude which each and every one of us has always carried with him, more inaccessible than the ice-cold mountains, more profound than the midnight sea; the solitude of self. Our inner being which we call ourself, no eye nor touch of man or angel has ever pierced, it is more hidden than the caves of the gnome; the sacred adytum[18] of the **oracle**;[19] the hidden chamber of Eleusinian mystery,[20] for to it only **omniscience**[21] is permitted to enter.

---

[15] **pecuniary**—monetary; financial.

[16] demoniac—possessed by a demon.

[17] base—contemptible; inferior; lacking in values or ethics.

[18] adytum—inner sanctuary of a temple admissible only to priests.

[19] **oracle**—shrine in which an ancient knowledge is revealed.

[20] Eleusinian mystery—religious mystery celebrated at the ancient Greek city of Eleusis in honor of Persephone and Demeter.

[21] **omniscience**—God's total knowledge.

Such is individual life. Who, I ask you, can take, dare take on himself the rights, the duties, the responsibilities of another human soul?

QUESTIONS TO CONSIDER

1. What does Stanton say is the strongest reason women should have a voice in government?

2. What is she saying when she compares a woman's life to that of a solitary voyager?

3. What are Stanton's arguments for giving women an education?

4. What part does the importance of individual responsibility play in Stanton's argument?

5. In your opinion, what would it take to devote your entire life to a cause that would not be completed in your lifetime? Is there a cause that you could feel that strongly about? Overall, do you think being a liberating voice for humanity is something that more people should be encouraged to do? Why or why not?

from

A Room of
One's Own

BY VIRGINIA WOOLF

*Novelist Virginia Woolf (1882–1941) is known for her experimental
novels, which use an internal stream of consciousness style to
divulge her characters' thoughts and emotions. Her book-length
essay,* A Room of One's Own *(1929), explores the difficulties
encountered by women writers in a man's world. This excerpt takes
place after the narrator has been to an extravagant lunch at the
fictional men's college, Oxbridge, where she was denied access to the
university library because she was not accompanied by a student
or professor (who would have been male). After a meager dinner at
the fictional women's college, Fernham, she talks with her friend
Mary about why women's colleges are so poor in comparison to
those of men. In response, Mary explains the difficulties women
face in raising money for the college.*

Well, said Mary Seton, about the year 1860—Oh, but
you know the story, she said, bored, I suppose, by the
recital. And she told me—rooms were hired.

Committees met. Envelopes were addressed. Circulars were drawn up. Meetings were held; letters were read out; so-and-so has promised so much; on the contrary, Mr. ___ won't give a penny. The *Saturday Review* has been very rude. How can we raise a fund to pay for offices? Shall we hold a bazaar? Can't we find a pretty girl to sit in the front row? Let us look up what John Stuart Mill[1] said on the subject. Can any one persuade the editor of the ___ to print a letter? Can we get Lady ___ to sign it? Lady ___ is out of town. That was the way it was done, presumably, sixty years ago, and it was a **prodigious**[2] effort, and a great deal of time was spent on it. And it was only after a long struggle and with the utmost difficulty that they got thirty thousand pounds together. So obviously we cannot have wine and partridges and servants carrying tin dishes on their heads, she said. We cannot have sofas and separate rooms. "The **amenities**,"[3] she said, quoting from some book or other, "will have to wait." At the thought of all those women working year after year and finding it hard to get two thousand pounds together, and as much as they could do to get thirty thousand pounds, we burst out in scorn at the **reprehensible**[4] poverty of our sex. What had our mothers been doing then that they had no wealth to leave us? Powdering their noses? Looking in at shop windows? Flaunting in the sun at Monte Carlo?[5] There were some photographs on the mantel-piece. Mary's mother—if that was her picture—may have been a

---

[1] John Stuart Mill (1807–1873) was a nineteenth-century English philosopher and economist. He wrote *The Subjection of Women* (1869) in support of women's suffrage.

[2] **prodigious**—enormous; marvelous.

[3] **amenities**—luxuries, comforts.

[4] **reprehensible**—deserving sharp criticism.

[5] Monte Carlo—part of the principality of Monaco on the French Riviera; known as a popular vacation spot for wealthy people.

wastrel[6] in her spare time (she had thirteen children by a minister of the church), but if so her gay and **dissipated**[7] life had left too few traces of its pleasures on her face. She was a homely body; an old lady in a plaid shawl which was fastened by a large cameo; and she sat in a basket-chair, encouraging a spaniel to look at the camera, with the amused, yet strained expression of one who is sure that the dog will move directly the bulb is pressed. Now if she had gone into business; had become a manufacturer of artificial silk or a **magnate**[8] on the Stock Exchange; if she had left two or three hundred thousand pounds to Fernham, we could have been sitting at our ease tonight and the subject of our talk might have been archaeology, botany, anthropology, physics, the nature of the atom, mathematics, astronomy, relativity, geography. If only Mrs. Seton and her mother and her mother before her had learnt the great art of making money and had left their money, like their fathers and their grandfathers before them, to found fellowships and lectureships and prizes and scholarships **appropriated**[9] to the use of their own sex, we might have dined very tolerably up here alone off a bird and a bottle of wine; we might have looked forward without undue confidence to a pleasant and honourable lifetime spent in the shelter of one of the liberally endowed professions.[10] We might have been exploring or writing; mooning about the **venerable**[11] places of the earth; sitting contemplative on the steps of the Parthenon, or going at ten to an office and coming home comfortably at half-past four to write a little poetry. Only, if Mrs. Seton and her like had gone into business at the age of fifteen, there would have

---

[6] **wastrel**—wasteful person; idle; good-for-nothing. Woolf is being sarcastic.

[7] **dissipated**—extravagant.

[8] **magnate**—person of great power and importance, especially in business.

[9] **appropriated**—taken, especially without permission.

[10] liberally endowed professions—well-paid jobs.

[11] **venerable**—deserving respect because of age or historic association.

been—that was the snag in the argument—no Mary. What, I asked, did Mary think of that? There between the curtains was the October night, calm and lovely, with a star or two caught in the yellowing trees. Was she ready to resign her share of it and her memories (for they had been a happy family, though a large one) of games and quarrels up in Scotland, which she is never tired of praising for the fineness of its air and the quality of its cakes, in order that Fernham might have been endowed with fifty thousand pounds or so by a stroke of the pen? For, to **endow**[12] a college would necessitate the **suppression**[13] of families altogether. Making a fortune and bearing thirteen children—no human being could stand it. Consider the facts, we said. First there are nine months before the baby is born. Then the baby is born. Then there are three or four months spent in feeding the baby. After the baby is fed there are certainly five years spent in playing with the baby. You cannot, it seems, let children run about the streets. People who have seen them running wild in Russia say that the sight is not a pleasant one. People say, too, that human nature takes its shape in the years between one and five. If Mrs. Seton, I said, had been making money, what sort of memories would you have had of games and quarrels? What would you have known of Scotland, and its fine air and cakes and all the rest of it? But it is useless to ask these questions, because you would never have come into existence at all. Moreover, it is equally useless to ask what might have happened if Mrs. Seton and her mother and her mother before her had **amassed**[14] great wealth and laid it under the foundations of college and library, because, in the first place, to earn money was impossible for them, and in the second, had it been possible, the law

---

[12] **endow**—make a gift of money or property as a source of permanent income.

[13] **suppression**—ending.

[14] **amassed**—collected; accumulated.

denied them the right to possess what money they earned. It is only for the last forty-eight years that Mrs. Seton has had a penny of her own. For all the centuries before that it would have been her husband's property—a thought which, perhaps, may have had its share in keeping Mrs. Seton and her mothers off the Stock Exchange. Every penny I earn, they may have said, will be taken from me and disposed of according to my husband's wisdom— perhaps to found a scholarship or to endow a fellowship in Balliol or Kings,[15] so that to earn money, even if I could earn money, is not a matter that interests me very greatly. I had better leave it to my husband.

At any rate, whether or not the blame rested on the old lady who was looking at the spaniel, there could be no doubt that for some reason or other our mothers had mismanaged their affairs very gravely. Not a penny could be spared for "amenities"; for partridges and wine, beadles[16] and turf, books and cigars, libraries and leisure. To raise bare walls out of the bare earth was the utmost they could do.

So we talked, standing at the window and looking, as so many thousands look every night, down on the domes and towers of the famous city beneath us. It was very beautiful, very mysterious in the autumn moonlight. The old stone looked very white and venerable. One thought of all the books that were assembled down there; of the pictures of old prelates[17] and worthies hanging in the paneled rooms; of the painted windows that would be throwing strange globes and crescents on the pavement; of the tablets and memorials and inscriptions; of the fountains and the grass; of the quiet rooms looking across the quiet quadrangles.[18] And (pardon me

---

[15] Balliol or Kings—men's colleges that are part of the English universities at Oxford and Cambridge.

[16] beadles—minor officials whose main duty is to keep order.

[17] prelates—bishops of superior rank.

[18] quadrangles—four-sided, often grassy, enclosures surrounded by buildings.

the thought) I thought, too, of the admirable smoke and drink and the deep armchairs and the pleasant carpets: of the **urbanity,**[19] the **geniality,**[20] the dignity which are the offspring of luxury and privacy and space. Certainly our mothers had not provided us with anything comparable to all this—our mothers who found it difficult to scrape together thirty thousand pounds, our mothers who bore thirteen children to ministers of religion at St. Andrews.[21]

---

[19] **urbanity**—sophistication.

[20] **geniality**—pleasant cheerfulness; friendliness.

[21] St. Andrews—a Scottish university.

QUESTIONS TO CONSIDER

1. What is the narrator's primary complaint?

2. What role or purpose does Mrs. Seton, Mary's mother, serve in Virginia Woolf's writing?

3. What do Woolf and Mary Seton believe to be the result if Mrs. Seton had been the kind of fund-raiser and activist they desired?

4. How would you explain the lack of funds for women's colleges in Woolf's day?

5. Why did Woolf feel that money was not of grave importance to women in that time?

The Problem That Has No Name

BY BETTY FRIEDAN

*Betty Friedan (1921–   ) grew up in Peoria, Illinois. After completing
graduate work in psychology and after her marriage and the
birth of her children, she became a free-lance writer.* The Feminine
Mystique, *published in 1963, ignited a revolution that changed
the lives of women throughout the world by jump-starting the women's
movement. Friedan went on to co-found and become the first
president of the National Organization for Women. She organized
the Women's Strike for Equality in 1970 and co-convened the
National Women's Political Caucus in 1971. In this selection from*
The Feminine Mystique, *Friedan addresses the problems that
women faced at home and in society at the time of her writing.*

The problem lay buried, unspoken, for many years
in the minds of American women. It was a strange stirring, a sense of dissatisfaction, a yearning that women
suffered in the middle of the twentieth century in the
United States. Each suburban wife struggled with it
alone. As she made the beds, shopped for groceries,

matched slipcover material, ate peanut butter sandwiches with her children, chauffeured Cub Scouts and Brownies, lay beside her husband at night—she was afraid to ask even of herself the silent question—"Is this all?"

For over fifteen years there was no word of this yearning in the millions of words written about women, for women, in all the columns, books and articles by experts telling women their role was to seek fulfillment as wives and mothers. Over and over women heard in voices of tradition and of Freudian[1] sophistication that they could desire no greater destiny than to glory in their own femininity. Experts told them how to catch a man and keep him, how to breastfeed children and handle their toilet training, how to cope with **sibling rivalry**[2] and adolescent rebellion; how to buy a dishwasher, bake bread, cook gourmet snails, and build a swimming pool with their own hands; how to dress, look, and act more feminine and make marriage more exciting; how to keep their husbands from dying young and their sons from growing into delinquents. They were taught to pity the neurotic, unfeminine, unhappy women who wanted to be poets or physicists or presidents. They learned that truly feminine women do not want careers, higher education, political rights—the independence and the opportunities that the old-fashioned feminists fought for. Some women, in their forties and fifties, still remembered painfully giving up those dreams, but most of the younger women no longer even thought about them. A thousand expert voices applauded their femininity, their adjustment, their new maturity. All they had to do was devote their lives from earliest girlhood to finding a husband and bearing children. . . .

The suburban housewife—she was the dream image of the young American women and the envy, it was said,

---

[1] Freudian—relating to the psychoanalytic theories of Sigmund Freud (1856–1939).

[2] **sibling rivalry**—competition between siblings (brothers and sisters).

of women all over the world. The American housewife—freed by science and labor-saving appliances from the **drudgery**,[3] the dangers of childbirth and the illnesses of her grandmother. She was healthy, beautiful, educated, concerned only about her husband, her children, her home. She had found true feminine fulfillment. As a housewife and mother, she was respected as a full and equal partner to man in his world. She was free to choose automobiles, clothes, appliances, supermarkets; she had everything that women ever dreamed of.

In the fifteen years after World War II, this **mystique**[4] of feminine fulfillment became the cherished and self-perpetuating core of contemporary American culture. Millions of women lived their lives in the image of those pretty pictures of the American suburban housewife, kissing their husbands goodbye in front of the picture window, depositing their station-wagonsful of children at school, and smiling as they ran the new electric waxer over the spotless kitchen floor. They baked their own bread, sewed their own and their children's clothes, kept their new washing machines and dryers running all day. They changed the sheets on the beds twice a week instead of once, took the rug-hooking class in adult education, and pitied their poor frustrated mothers, who had dreamed of having a career. Their only dream was to be perfect wives and mothers; their highest ambition to have five children and a beautiful house, their only fight to get and keep their husbands. They had no thought for the unfeminine problems of the world outside the home; they wanted the men to make the major decisions. They gloried in their role as women, and wrote proudly on the census blank: "Occupation: housewife." . . .

If a woman had a problem in the 1950's and 1960's, she knew that something must be wrong with her marriage, or with herself. Other women were satisfied with their

---

[3] **drudgery**—dull, tiring work.

[4] **mystique**—mysterious attitude developing around something.

lives, she thought. What kind of a woman was she if she did not feel this mysterious fulfillment waxing the kitchen floor? She was so ashamed to admit her dissatisfaction that she never knew how many other women shared it. If she tried to tell her husband, he didn't understand what she was talking about. She did not really understand it herself. For over fifteen years women in America found it harder to talk about this problem than about sex. Even the psychoanalysts had no name for it. When a woman went to a psychiatrist for help, as many women did, she would say, "I'm so ashamed," or "I must be hopelessly neurotic." "I don't know what's wrong with women today," a suburban psychiatrist said uneasily. "I only know something is wrong because most of my patients happen to be women. And their problem isn't sexual." Most women with this problem did not go to see a psychoanalyst, however. "There's nothing wrong really," they kept telling themselves. "There isn't any problem."

But on an April morning in 1959, I heard a mother of four, having coffee with four other mothers in a suburban development fifteen miles from New York say in a tone of quiet desperation, "the problem." And the others knew, without words, that she was not talking about a problem with her husband, or her children, or her home. Suddenly they realized they all shared the same problem, the problem that has no name. They began, hesitantly, to talk about it. Later, after they had picked up their children at nursery school and taken them home to nap, two of the women cried, in sheer relief, just to know they were not alone.

Gradually I came to realize that the problem that has no name was shared by countless women in America. As a magazine writer I often interviewed women about problems with their children, or their marriages, or their houses, or their communities. But after a while I began to recognize the telltale signs of this other problem. I saw the same signs in suburban ranch houses and split-levels[5] on Long Island and in New Jersey and Westchester County; in colonial houses in a small Massachusetts town; on patios in Memphis; in suburban and city apartments; in living rooms in the Midwest. Sometimes I sensed the problem, not as a reporter, but as a suburban housewife, for during this time I was also bringing up my own three children in Rockland County, New York. I heard echoes of the problem in college dormitories and semi-private maternity wards,[6] at PTA meetings and luncheons of the League of Women Voters, at suburban cocktail parties, in station wagons waiting for trains, and in snatches of conversation overheard at Schrafft's. The groping words I heard from other women, on quiet afternoons when children were at school or on quiet evenings when husbands worked late, I think I understood first as a woman long before I understood their larger social and psychological implications.

Just what was this problem that has no name? What were the words women used when they tried to express it? Sometimes a woman would say "I feel empty somehow . . . incomplete." Or she would say, "I feel as if I don't exist." Sometimes she blotted out the feeling with a tranquilizer. Sometimes she thought the problem was with her husband, or her children, or that what she really needed was to redecorate her house, or move to a better neighborhood, or have an affair, or another baby. Sometimes, she went to a doctor with symptoms she could hardly describe: "A tired feeling . . . I get so angry with the children it scares me . . . I feel like crying without any reason." (A Cleveland doctor called it "the housewife's syndrome.") A number of women told me about great bleeding blisters that break out on their hands and arms. "I call it the housewife's blight," said a family doctor in Pennsylvania. "I see it so often lately in

---

[5] split-levels—houses with different levels.

[6] maternity wards—areas in a hospital where women recover after childbirth.

these young women with four, five and six children who bury themselves in their dishpans. But it isn't caused by detergent and it isn't cured by cortisone."[7] . . .

In 1960, the problem that has no name burst like a boil through the image of the happy American housewife. In the television commercials the pretty housewives still beamed over their foaming dishpans and *Time's* cover story on "The Suburban Wife, an American Phenomenon" protested: "Having too good a time . . . to believe that they should be unhappy." But the actual unhappiness of the American housewife was suddenly being reported—from the *New York Times* to *Newsweek* to *Good Housekeeping* and CBS Television ("The Trapped Housewife"), although almost everybody who talked about it found some superficial reason to dismiss it. It was attributed to incompetent appliance repairmen (*New York Times*), or the distances children must be chauffeured in the suburbs (*Time*) or too much PTA (*Redbook*). Some said it was the old problem—education: more and more women had education, which naturally made them unhappy in their role as housewives. "The road from Freud to Frigidaire,[8] from Sophocles[9] to Spock,[10] has turned out to be a bumpy one," reported the *New York Times* (June 28, 1960). "Many young women—certainly not all—whose education plunged them into a world of ideas feel **stifled**[11] in their homes. They find their routine lives out of joint with their training. Like shut-ins, they feel left out. In the last year, the problem of the educated housewife has provided the meat of dozens of speeches made by troubled presidents of women's colleges who maintain, in the face of complaints, that sixteen years of academic training is realistic preparation for wifehood and motherhood."

---

[7] cortisone—a topical cream used to treat skin inflammations.

[8] Frigidaire—brand name of a refrigerator.

[9] Sophocles (496–406 B.C.)—ancient Greek dramatist.

[10] Spock—Dr. Benjamin Spock (1903–1998) pediatrician whose book *Baby and Child Care* guided millions of parents.

[11] **stifled**—suffocated, smothered.

There was much sympathy for the educated housewife. ("Like a two-headed schizophrenic . . . once she wrote a paper on the Graveyard poets; now she writes notes to the milkman. Once she determined the boiling point of sulphuric acid; now she determines her boiling point with the overdue repairman. . . . The housewife often is reduced to screams and tears. . . . No one, it seems, is appreciative, least of all herself, of the kind of person she becomes in the process of turning from poetess into **shrew**."[12])

Home economists suggested more realistic preparation for housewives, such as high-school workshops in home appliances. College educators suggested more discussion groups on home management and the family, to prepare women for the adjustment to domestic life. A **spate**[13] of articles appeared in the mass magazines offering "Fifty-eight Ways to Make Your Marriage More Exciting." No month went by without a new book by a psychiatrist or sexologist offering technical advice on finding greater fulfillment through sex.

A male humorist joked in *Harper's Bazaar* (July, 1960) that the problem could be solved by taking away woman's right to vote. ("In the pre-19th Amendment era, the American woman was **placid**,[14] sheltered and sure of her role in American society. She left all the political decisions to her husband and he, in turn, left all the family decisions to her. Today a woman has to make both the family *and* the political decisions, and it's too much for her.")

A number of educators suggested seriously that women no longer be admitted to the four-year colleges and universities: in the growing college crisis, the education which girls could not use as housewives was more urgently needed than ever by boys to do the work of the atomic age.

The problem was also dismissed with drastic solutions no one could take seriously. (A woman writer proposed in

---

[12] **shrew**—ill-tempered woman.

[13] **spate**—large number.

[14] **placid**—quiet, calm.

Harper's that women be drafted for compulsory service as nurses' aides and baby-sitters.) And it was smoothed over with the age-old **panaceas**:[15] "love is their answer," "the only answer is inner help," "the secret of completeness—children," "a private means of intellectual fulfillment," "to cure this toothache of the spirit—the simple formula of handing one's self and one's will over to God."

The problem was dismissed by telling the housewife she doesn't realize how lucky she is—her own boss, no time clock, no junior executive gunning for her job. What if she isn't happy—does she think men are happy in this world? Does she really, secretly, still want to be a man? Doesn't she know yet how lucky she is to be a woman? . . .

Even so, most men, and some women, still did not know that this problem was real. But those who had faced it honestly knew that all the superficial remedies, the sympathetic advice, the scolding words and the cheering words were somehow drowning the problem in unreality. A bitter laugh was beginning to be heard from American women. They were admired, envied, pitied, theorized over until they were sick of it, offered drastic solutions or silly choices that no one could take seriously. They got all kinds of advice from the growing armies of marriage and child-guidance counselors, psychotherapists, and armchair psychologists,[16] on how to adjust to their role as housewives. No other road to fulfillment was offered to American women in the middle of the twentieth century. Most adjusted to their role and suffered or ignored the problem that has no name. It can be less painful for a woman, not to hear the strange, dissatisfied voice stirring within her.

It is no longer possible to ignore that voice, to dismiss the desperation of so many American women. This is not what being a woman means, no matter what the experts say. For human suffering there is a reason; perhaps

---

[15] **panaceas**—cure-alls.

[16] armchair psychologists—amateur psychologists.

the reason has not been found because the right questions have not been asked, or pressed far enough. I do not accept the answer that there is no problem because American women have luxuries that women in other times and lands never dreamed of; part of the strange newness of the problem is that it cannot be understood in terms of the age-old material problems of man: poverty, sickness, hunger, cold. The women who suffer this problem have a hunger that food cannot fill. . . .

Can the problem that has no name be somehow related to the domestic routine of the housewife? When a woman tries to put the problem into words, she often merely describes the daily life she leads. What is there in this recital of comfortable domestic detail that could possibly cause such a feeling of desperation? Is she trapped simply by the enormous demands of her role as modern housewife: wife, mistress, mother, nurse, consumer, cook, chauffeur; expert on interior decoration, child care, appliance repair, furniture refinishing, nutrition, and education? Her day is fragmented as she rushes from dishwasher to washing machine to telephone to dryer to station wagon to supermarket and delivers Johnny to the Little League field, takes Janey to dancing class, gets the lawnmower fixed and meets the 6:45. She can never spend more than 15 minutes on any one thing; she has no time to read books, only magazines; even if she had time, she has lost the power to concentrate. At the end of the day, she is so terribly tired that sometimes her husband has to take over and put the children to bed.

Thus terrible tiredness took so many women to doctors in the 1950's that one decided to investigate it. He found, surprisingly, that his patients suffering from "housewife's fatigue" slept more than an adult needed to sleep—as much as ten hours a day—and that the actual energy expended on housework did not tax their capacity. The real problem must be something else, he decided—perhaps boredom. Some doctors told their women patients they must get out of the house for a day, treat themselves to a movie in town. Others prescribed tranquilizers. Many suburban housewives were taking tranquilizers like cough drops. "You wake up in the morning, and you feel as if there's no point in going on another day like this. So you take a tranquilizer because it makes you not care so much that it's pointless."

It is easy to see the concrete details that trap the suburban housewife, the continual demands on her time. But the chains that bind her in her trap are chains in her own mind and spirit. They are chains made up of mistaken ideas and misinterpreted facts, of incomplete truths and unreal choices. They are not easily seen and not easily shaken off.

How can any woman see the whole truth within the bounds of her own life? How can she believe that voice inside herself, when it denies the conventional, accepted truths by which she has been living? And yet the women I have talked to, who are finally listening to that inner voice, seem in some incredible way to be groping through to a truth that has defied the experts.

QUESTIONS TO CONSIDER

1. How would you summarize the problem Friedan addresses in this excerpt? Why do you think the problem has no name? What would you name it?

2. What is the feminine role Friedan exposes? What does she see as the problem with such a distorted image of femininity?

3. What were some of the symptoms of the deep frustration and unhappiness felt by many women with this role? How did increased educational opportunities for women make the problem worse?

4. What has changed, in your view, from what Friedan described? What issues remain? Overall, what do you observe about the lives of women today?

NOW Bill of Rights

BY THE NATIONAL ORGANIZATION
FOR WOMEN

The National Organization for Women (NOW) was formed in 1966 by Betty Friedan and thirty other legislators, authors, professionals, labor workers, and academics. Betty Friedan, author of The Feminine Mystique, *served as its first president. Among the issues NOW addressed through lobbying and litigation were child care, job discrimination, equal educational opportunities for women, and reproductive rights. NOW's major concern in the 1970s and early 1980s was securing passage of the Equal Rights Amendment (ERA) to the Constitution. However, the amendment failed to gain ratification by the required number of states in 1982. NOW's platform, included here, outlines the main issues addressed by the organization.*

Bill of Rights
National Organization for Women (NOW)

  I Equal Rights Constitutional Amendment

 II Enforce Law Banning Sex Discrimination in Employment

III Maternity Leave Rights in Employment and in Social Security Benefits

IV Tax Deduction for Home and Child Care Expenses for Working Parents

V Child Care Centers

VI Equal and Unsegregated Education

VII Equal Job Training Opportunities and Allowances for Women in Poverty

VIII The Right of Women to Control Their Reproductive Lives

WE DEMAND
Exception

I

That the United States Congress immediately pass the Equal Rights Amendment to the Constitution to provide that "Equality of rights under the law shall not be denied or abridged by the United States or by any State on account of sex," and that such then be immediately ratified by the several States.

II

That equal employment opportunity be guaranteed to all women, as well as men, by insisting that the Equal Employment Opportunity Commission enforces the prohibitions against sex discrimination in employment under Title VII of the Civil Rights Act of 1964 with the same vigor as it enforces the prohibitions against racial discrimination.

III

That women be protected by law to ensure their rights to return to their jobs within a reasonable time after childbirth without loss of seniority or other accrued benefits,[1] and be paid maternity leave as a form of social security and/or employee benefit.

---

[1] accrued benefits—earned rewards that increase over time.

IV

Immediate revision of tax laws to permit the deduction of home and child care expenses for working parents.

V

That child care facilities be established by law on the same basis as parks, libraries, and public schools, adequate to the needs of children from pre-school years through adolescence, as a community resource to be used by all citizens from all income levels.

VI

That the right of women to be educated to their potential full equally with men be secured by Federal and State Legislation, eliminating all discrimination and segregation by sex, written and unwritten, at all levels of education, including colleges, graduate and professional schools, loans and fellowships, and Federal and State training programs such as the Job Corps.

VII

The right of women in poverty to secure job training, housing, and family allowances on equal terms with men, but without prejudice to a parent's right to remain at home to care for his or her children; revision of welfare legislation and poverty programs which deny women dignity, privacy, and self-respect.

VIII

The right of women to control their own reproductive lives by removing from penal codes laws limiting access to contraceptive information and devices and laws governing abortion.

QUESTIONS TO CONSIDER

1. Why do you think the National Organization for Women was seen by many women (and men) to be necessary?

2. What is your opinion of the NOW Bill of Rights?

3. From the perspective of today, which demands by NOW seem the most radical? Why?

4. Which of the items in the NOW Bill of Rights seem to have been attained? Which rights still have yet to be attained? Why do you think this is?

5. Why do you think NOW felt that the rights of women spelled out in the ERA were not addressed sufficiently in the Constitution? What, in your view, may be the reason the amendment failed to be ratified?

I Stand Here Ironing

BY TILLIE OLSEN

Tillie Olsen (1913–   ) was the daughter of Russian immigrants active in the labor movement. She grew up in Nebraska and dropped out of school after the eleventh grade. Taking work in the meat-packing houses in Kansas City and concerned about the working conditions she found there, Olsen attempted to organize the packing house workers, which led to her arrest and jail. She began writing her first novel, Yonnondio: From the Thirties, *when she was nineteen, but working and raising a family kept her from completing it for many years. Then, in 1955, she won a fellowship at Stanford University that let her focus on her writing. In addition to* Yonnondio, *her works include* Silence *and the short story collection* Tell Me a Riddle, *the title story of which won the 1961 O. Henry Award for best American short story of the year. Olsen's writings are concerned with the distractions and pressures that keep women from leading fulfilled lives. In the following story from* Tell Me a Riddle, *Olsen's narrator reminisces about the struggles and heartaches of raising her children as an impoverished single mother.*

I stand here ironing, and what you asked me moves tormented back and forth with the iron.

"I wish you would manage the time to come in and talk with me about your daughter. I'm sure you can help me understand her. She's a youngster who needs help and whom I'm deeply interested in helping."

"Who needs help." . . . Even if I came, what good would it do? You think because I am her mother I have a key, or that in some way you could use me as a key? She has lived for nineteen years. There is all that life that has happened outside of me, beyond me.

And when is there time to remember, to sift, to weigh, to estimate, to total? I will start and there will be an interruption and I will have to gather it all together again. Or I will become engulfed with all I did or did not do, with what should have been and what cannot be helped.

She was a beautiful baby. The first and only one of our five that was beautiful at birth. You do not guess how new and uneasy her tenancy[1] in her now-loveliness. You did not know her all those years she was thought homely, or see her poring over her baby pictures, making me tell her over and over how beautiful she had been—and would be, I would tell her—and was now, to the seeing eye. But the seeing eyes were few or non-existent. Including mine.

I nursed her. They feel that's important nowadays. I nursed all the children, but with her, with all the fierce rigidity of first motherhood, I did like the books then said. Though her cries battered me to trembling and my breasts ached with swollenness, I waited till the clock decreed.

Why do I put that first? I do not even know if it matters, or if it explains anything.

She was a beautiful baby. She blew shining bubbles of sound. She loved motion, loved light, loved color and music and textures. She would lie on the floor in her blue overalls patting the surface so hard in ecstasy her hands and feet would blur. She was a miracle to me, but when she was eight months old I had to leave her daytimes

---

[1] tenancy—occupying, living in.

with the woman downstairs to whom she was no miracle at all, for I worked or looked for work and for Emily's father, who "could no longer endure" (he wrote in his good-bye note) "sharing want with us."

I was nineteen. It was the pre-relief, pre-WPA[2] world of the depression. I would start running as soon as I got off the streetcar, running up the stairs, the place smelling sour, and awake or asleep to startle awake, when she saw me she would break into a clogged weeping that could not be comforted, a weeping I can hear yet.

After a while I found a job **hashing**[3] at night so I could be with her days, and it was better. But it came to where I had to bring her to his family and leave her.

It took a long time to raise the money for her fare back. Then she got chicken pox and I had to wait longer. When she finally came, I hardly knew her, walking quick and nervous like her father, looking like her father, thin, and dressed in a shoddy red that yellowed her skin and glared at the pockmarks. All the baby loveliness gone.

She was two. Old enough for nursery school they said, and I did not know then what I know now—the fatigue of the long day, and the **lacerations**[4] of group life in the kinds of nurseries that are only parking places for children.

Except that it would have made no difference if I had known. It was the only place there was. It was the only way we could be together, the only way I could hold a job.

And even without knowing, I knew. I knew the teacher that was evil because all these years it has curdled into my memory, the little boy hunched in the corner, her rasp, "why aren't you outside, because Alvin hits you? that's no reason, go out, scaredy." I knew Emily hated it even if she did not clutch and implore "don't go Mommy" like the other children, mornings.

---

[2] pre-WPA—before the Work Projects Administration, a federal program established in 1935 to provide employment during the Great Depression.

[3] **hashing**—cooking in a restaurant or diner.

[4] **lacerations**—wounds.

She always had a reason why we should stay home. Momma, you look sick, Momma. I feel sick. Momma, the teachers aren't there today, they're sick. Momma, we can't go, there was a fire there last night. Momma, it's a holiday today, no school, they told me.

But never a direct protest, never rebellion. I think of our others in their three-, four-year-oldness—the explosions, the tempers, the **denunciations,**[5] the demands—and I feel suddenly ill. I put the iron down. What in me demanded that goodness in her? And what was the cost, the cost to her of such goodness?

The old man living in the back once said in his gentle way: "You should smile at Emily more when you look at her." What *was* in my face when I looked at her? I loved her. There were all the acts of love.

It was only with the others I remembered what he said, and it was the face of joy, and not of care or tightness or worry I turned to them—too late for Emily. She does not smile easily, let alone almost always as her brothers and sisters do. Her face is closed and **sombre,**[6] but when she wants, how fluid. You must have seen it in her **pantomimes,**[7] you spoke of her rare gift for comedy on the stage that rouses a laughter out of the audience so dear they applaud and applaud and do not want to let her go.

Where does it come from, that comedy? There was none of it in her when she came back to me that second time, after I had had to send her away again. She had a new daddy now to learn to love, and I think perhaps it was a better time.

Except when we left her alone nights, telling ourselves she was old enough.

"Can't you go some other time, Mommy, like tomorrow?" she would ask. "Will it be just a little while you'll be gone? Do you promise?"

---

[5] **denunciations**—criticisms.

[6] **sombre**—somber; serious.

[7] **pantomines**—silent dramatic or dancing performances.

The time we came back, the front door open, the clock on the floor in the hall. She rigid awake. "It wasn't just a little while. I didn't cry. Three times I called you, just three times, and then I ran downstairs, to open the door so you could come faster. The clock talked loud. I threw it away, it scared me what it talked."

She said the clock talked loud again that night I went to the hospital to have Susan. She was delirious with the fever that comes before red measles, but she was fully conscious all the week I was gone and the week after we were home when she could not come near the new baby or me.

She did not get well. She stayed skeleton thin, not wanting to eat; and night after night she had nightmares. She would call for me, and I would rouse from exhaustion to sleepily call back: "You're all right, darling, go to sleep, it's just a dream," and if she still called, in a sterner voice, "now go to sleep, Emily, there's nothing to hurt you." Twice, only twice, when I had to get up for Susan anyhow, I went in to sit with her.

Now when it is too late (as if she would let me hold and comfort her like I do the others) I get up and go to her at once at her moan or restless stirring. "Are you awake, Emily? Can I get you something?" And the answer is always the same: "No, I'm all right, go back to sleep, Mother."

They persuaded me at the clinic to send her away to a convalescent home in the country where "she can have the kind of food and care you can't manage for her, and you'll be free to concentrate on the new baby." They still send children to that place. I see pictures on the society page of sleek young women planning affairs to raise money for it, or dancing at the affairs, or decorating Easter eggs or filling Christmas stockings for the children.

They never have a picture of the children so I do not know if the girls still wear those gigantic red bows and the ravaged looks on the every other Sunday when parents can come to visit "unless otherwise notified"—as we were notified the first six weeks.

Oh it is a handsome place, green lawns and tall trees and fluted flower beds. High up on the balconies of each cottage the children stand, the girls in their red bows and white dresses, the boys in white suits and giant red ties. The parents stand below shrieking up to be heard and the children shriek down to be heard, and between them the invisible wall "Not To Be Contaminated by Parental Germs or Physical Affection."

There was a tiny girl who always stood hand in hand with Emily. Her parents never came. One visit she was gone. "They moved her to Rose Cottage," Emily shouted in explanation. "They don't like you to love anybody here."

She wrote once a week, the labored writing of a seven-year-old. "I am fine. How is the baby. If I write my leter nicly I will have a star. Love." There never was a star. We wrote every other day, letters she could never hold or keep but only hear read—once. "We simply do not have room for children to keep any personal possessions," they patiently explained when we pieced one Sunday's shrieking together to plead how much it would mean to Emily, who loved so to keep things, to be allowed to keep her letters and cards.

Each visit she looked frailer. "She isn't eating," they told us.

(They had runny eggs for breakfast or mush with lumps, Emily said later, I'd hold it in my mouth and not swallow. Nothing ever tasted good, just when they had chicken.)

It took us eight months to get her released home, and only the fact that she gained back so little of her seven lost pounds convinced the social worker.

I used to try to hold and love her after she came back, but her body would stay stiff, and after a while she'd push away. She ate little. Food sickened her, and I think much of life too. Oh she had physical lightness and brightness, twinkling by on skates, bouncing like a ball up and down up and down over the jump rope, skimming over the hill; but these were momentary.

She fretted about her appearance, thin and dark and foreign-looking at a time when every little girl was supposed to look or thought she should look a chubby blonde replica of Shirley Temple. The doorbell sometimes rang for her, but no one seemed to come and play in the house or be a best friend. Maybe because we moved so much.

There was a boy she loved painfully through two school semesters. Months later she told me how she had taken pennies from my purse to buy him candy. "Licorice was his favorite and I brought him some every day, but he still liked Jennifer better'n me. Why, Mommy?" The kind of question for which there is no answer.

School was a worry to her. She was not **glib**[8] or quick in a world where glibness and quickness were easily confused with ability to learn. To her overworked and exasperated teachers she was an **overconscientious**[9] "slow learner" who kept trying to catch up and was absent entirely too often.

I let her be absent, though sometimes the illness was imaginary. How different from my now-strictness about attendance with the others. I wasn't working. We had a new baby, I was home anyhow. Sometimes, after Susan grew old enough, I would keep her home from school, too, to have them all together.

Mostly, Emily had asthma, and her breathing, harsh and labored, would fill the house with a curiously **tranquil**[10] sound. I would bring the two old dresser mirrors and her boxes of collections to her bed. She would select beads and single earrings, bottle tops and shells; dried flowers and pebbles, old postcards and

---

[8] **glib**—at ease or fluent in speaking or writing.

[9] **overconscientious**—too careful, meticulous.

[10] **tranquil**—peaceful.

scraps, all sorts of oddments; then she and Susan would play Kingdom, setting up landscapes and furniture, peopling them with action.

Those were the only times of peaceful companionship between her and Susan. I have edged away from it, that poisonous feeling between them, that terrible balancing of hurts and needs I had to do between the two, and did so badly, those earlier years.

Oh there are conflicts between the others too, each one human, needing, demanding, hurting, taking—but only between Emily and Susan, no, Emily toward Susan that corroding resentment.[11] It seems so obvious on the surface, yet it is not obvious. Susan, the second child, Susan, golden- and curly-haired and chubby, quick and articulate and assured, everything in appearance and manner Emily was not; Susan, not able to resist Emily's precious things, losing or sometimes clumsily breaking them; Susan telling jokes and riddles to company for applause while Emily sat silent (to say to me later: that was *my* riddle, Mother, I told it to Susan); Susan, who for all the five years' difference in age was just a year behind Emily in developing physically.

I am glad for that slow physical development that widened the difference between her and her **contemporaries,**[12] though she suffered over it. She was too vulnerable for that terrible world of youthful competition, of **preening**[13] and parading, of constant measuring of yourself against every other, of envy, "If I had that copper hair," "If I had that skin. . . ." She tormented herself enough about not looking like the others, there was enough of the unsureness, the having to be conscious of words before you speak, the constant caring—what are they thinking of me? without having it all magnified by the merciless physical drives.

---

[11] corroding resentment—gnawing hatred or jealousy.

[12] **contemporaries**—friends; peers.

[13] **preening**—primping, gloating.

Ronnie is calling. He is wet and I change him. It is rare there is such a cry now. That time of motherhood is almost behind me when the ear is not one's own but must always be racked and listening for the child cry, the child call. We sit for a while and I hold him, looking out over the city spread in charcoal with its soft aisles of light. "*Shoogily*," he breathes and curls closer. I carry him back to bed, asleep. *Shoogily*. A funny word, a family word, inherited from Emily, invented by her to say: *comfort*.

In this and other ways she leaves her seal, I say aloud. And startle at my saying it. What do I mean? What did I start to gather together, to try and make coherent? I was at the terrible, growing years. War years. I do not remember them well. I was working, there were four smaller ones now, there was not time for her. She had to help be a mother, and housekeeper, and shopper. She had to set her seal. Mornings of crisis and near hysteria trying to get lunches packed, hair combed, coats and shoes found, everyone to school or Child Care on time, the baby ready for transportation. And always the paper scribbled on by a smaller one, the book looked at by Susan then mislaid, the homework not done. Running out to that huge school where she was one, she was lost, she was a drop; suffering over the unpreparedness, stammering and unsure in her classes.

There was so little time left at night after the kids were bedded down. She would struggle over books, always eating (it was in those years she developed her enormous appetite that is legendary in our family) and I would be ironing, or preparing food for the next day, or writing V-mail[14] to Bill, or tending the baby. Sometimes, to make me laugh, or out of her despair, she would imitate happenings or types at school.

I think I said once: "Why don't you do something like this in the school amateur show?" One morning she

---

[14] V-mail—Victory mail, letters sent by a mail system used by U.S. armed forces during World War II.

phoned me at work, hardly understandable through the weeping: "Mother, I did it. I won, I won; they gave me first prize; they clapped and clapped and wouldn't let me go."

Now suddenly she was Somebody, and as imprisoned in her difference as she had been in **anonymity.**[15]

She began to be asked to perform at other high schools, even in colleges, then at city and statewide affairs. The first one we went to, I only recognized her that first moment when thin, shy, she almost drowned herself into the curtains. Then: Was this Emily? The control, the command, the convulsing and deadly clowning, the spell, then the roaring, stamping audience, unwilling to let this rare and precious laughter out of their lives.

Afterwards: You ought to do something about her with a gift like that—but without money or knowing how, what does one do? We have left it all to her, and the gift has as often **eddied**[16] inside, clogged and clotted, as been used and growing.

She is coming. She runs up the stairs two at a time with her light graceful step, and I know she is happy tonight. Whatever it was that occasioned your call did not happen today.

"Aren't you ever going to finish the ironing, Mother? Whistler[17] painted his mother in a rocker. I'd have to paint mine standing over an ironing board." This is one of her communicative nights and she tells me everything and nothing as she fixes herself a plate of food out of the icebox.

She is so lovely. Why did you want me to come in at all? Why were you concerned? She will find her way.

She starts up the stairs to bed. "Don't get me up with the rest in the morning." "But I thought you were having midterms." "Oh, those," she comes back in, kisses

---

[15] **anonymity**—the state of being unknown, unacknowledged.

[16] **eddied**—run opposite to the current or flow, as in a whirlpool.

[17] Whistler—James McNeill Whistler (1834–1903) whose painting "Arrangement in Black and Grey No. 1: The Artist's Mother" is very famous.

me, and says quite lightly, "in a couple of years when we'll all be atom-dead they won't matter a bit."

She has said it before. She *believes* it. But because I have been dredging the past, and all that compounds a human being is so heavy and meaningful in me, I cannot endure it tonight.

I will never total it all. I will never come in to say: She was a child seldom smiled at. Her father left me before she was a year old. I had to work her first six years when there was work, or I sent her home and to his relatives. There were years she had care she hated. She was dark and thin and foreign-looking in a world where the prestige went to blondeness and curly hair and dimples, she was slow where glibness was prized. She was a child of anxious, not proud, love. We were poor and could not afford for her the soil of easy growth. I was a young mother, I was a distracted mother. There were the other children pushing up, demanding. Her younger sister seemed all that she was not. There were years she did not want me to touch her. She kept too much in herself, her life was such she had to keep too much in herself. My wisdom came too late. She has much to her and probably little will come of it. She is a child of her age, of depression, of war, of fear.

Let her be. So all that is in her will not bloom—but in how many does it? There is still enough left to live by. Only help her to know—help make it so there is cause for her to know—that she is more than this dress on the ironing board, helpless before the iron.

QUESTIONS TO CONSIDER

1. What challenges did this mother face in raising Emily?

2. How many of her issues are addressed in the NOW Bill of Rights? How might her life have been different if that bill had been law when Emily was born?

3. Why is the story called "I Stand Here Ironing"? What does this act signify?

May's Lion

BY URSULA K. LE GUIN

*Ursula K. Le Guin (1929–   ) is most well known for her science
fiction and fantasy novels, although she has also published poems
and essays. Her novels frequently contain societies with rules
different from those we know. In these societies, Le Guin demon-
strates how our views are shaped by laws and how we might have
developed differently. Le Guin's novels include* The Left Hand of
Darkness, The Dispossessed *(both of which won the Nebula
and Hugo Awards for science fiction), and* Always Coming Home.
In this next story, taken from a collection of short stories called
Buffalo Gals and Other Animal Presences *(1987), the narrator
liberates an old woman's voice, retelling her story to reveal a
broader, more encompassing meaning.*

Jim remembers it as a bobcat,[1] and he was May's
nephew, and ought to know. It probably was a bobcat.
I don't think May would have changed her story,
though you can't trust a good story-teller not to make
the story suit herself, or get the facts to fit the story better.
Anyhow she told it to us more than once, because my

---

[1] bobcat—wildcat.

mother and I would ask for it; and the way I remember it, it was a mountain lion. And the way I remember May telling it is sitting on the edge of the irrigation tank[2] we used to swim in, cement rough as a lava flow and hot in the sun, the long cracks tarred over. She was an old lady then with a long Irish upper lip, kind and **wary**[3] and **balky**.[4] She liked to come sit and talk with my mother while I swam; she didn't have all that many people to talk to. She always had chickens, in the chickenhouse very near the back door of the farmhouse, so the whole place smelled pretty strong of chickens, and as long as she could she kept a cow or two down in the old barn by the creek. The first of May's cows I remember was Pearl, a big handsome Holstein who gave fourteen or twenty-four or forty gallons or quarts of milk at a milking, whichever is right for a prize milker. Pearl was beautiful in my eyes when I was four or five years old; I loved and admired her. I remember how excited I was, how I reached upward to them, when Pearl or the workhorse Prince, for whom my love amounted to worship, would put an immense and sensitive muzzle through the three-strand fence to whisk a cornhusk from my fearful hand; and then the munching and the sweet breath and the big nose would be at the barbed wire again: the offering is acceptable. . . . After Pearl there was Rosie, a purebred Jersey. May got her either cheap or free because she was a runt[5] calf, so tiny that May brought her home on her lap in the back of the car, like a fawn. And Rosie always looked like she had some deer in her. She was a lovely, clever little cow and even more willful than old May. She often chose not to come in to be milked. We would hear May calling and then see her trudging across our lower pasture with the bucket, going to find Rosie wherever Rosie had decided to be

---

[2] irrigation tank—holding tank for water.

[3] **wary**—cautious.

[4] **balky**—given to refusing to proceed.

[5] runt—smallest of the calves born together in a litter; stunted.

milked today on the wild hills she had to roam in, a hundred acres of our and Old Jim's land. Then May had a fox terrier named Pinky, who yipped and nipped and turned me against fox terriers for life, but he was long gone when the mountain lion came; and the black cats who lived in the barn kept discreetly out of the story. As a matter of fact now I think of it the chickens weren't in it either. It might have been quite different if they had been. May had quit keeping chickens after old Mrs. Walter died. It was just her all alone there, and Rosie and the cats down in the barn, and nobody else within sight or sound of the old farm. We were in our house up the hill only in the summer, and Jim lived in town, those years. What time of year it was I don't know, but I imagine the grass still green or just turning gold. And May was in the house, in the kitchen, where she lived entirely unless she was asleep or outdoors, when she heard this noise.

Now you need May herself, sitting skinny on the edge of the irrigation tank, seventy or eighty or ninety years old, nobody knew how old May was and she had made sure they couldn't find out, opening her pleated[6] lips and letting out this noise—a huge, awful yowl, starting soft with a nasal hum and rising slowly into a snarling gargle that sank away into a sobbing purr. . . . It got better every time she told the story.

"It was some meow," she said.

So she went to the kitchen door, opened it, and looked out. Then she shut the kitchen door and went to the kitchen window to look out, because there was a mountain lion under the fig tree.

Puma, cougar, catamount;[7] *Felis concolor*,[8] the shy, secret, shadowy lion of the New World, four or five feet long plus a yard of black-tipped tail, weighs about what a woman weighs, lives where the deer live from Canada

---

[6] pleated—with even folds throughout.

[7] puma, cougar, catamount—various wildcats.

[8] *Felis concolor*—Latin for *cougar* or *wildcat*.

to Chile, but always shyer, always fewer, the color of dry leaves, dry grass.

There were plenty of deer in the Valley in the forties, but no mountain lion had been seen for decades anywhere near where people lived. Maybe way back up in the canyons; but Jim, who hunted, and knew every deer-trail in the hills, had never seen a lion. Nobody had, except May, now, alone in her kitchen.

"I thought maybe it was sick," she told us. "It wasn't acting right. I don't think a lion would walk right into the yard like that if it was feeling well. If I'd still had the chickens it'd be a different story maybe! But it just walked around some, and then it lay down there," and she points between the fig tree and the **decrepit**[9] garage. "And then after a while it kind of meowed again, and got up and come into the shade right there." The fig tree, planted when the house was built, about the time May was born, makes a great, green, sweet-smelling shade. "It just laid there looking around. It wasn't well," says May.

She had lived with and looked after animals all her life; she had also earned her living for years as a nurse.

"Well, I didn't know exactly what to do for it. So I put out some water for it. It didn't even get up when I come out the door. I put the water down there, not so close to it that we'd scare each other, see, and it kept watching me, but it didn't move. After I went back in it did get up and tried to drink some water. Then it made that kind of meowowow. I do believe it come here because it was looking for help. Or just for company, maybe."

The afternoon went on, May in the kitchen, the lion under the fig tree.

But down in the barnyard by the creek was Rosie the cow. Fortunately the gate was shut, so she could not

---

[9] **decrepit**—broken down; made feeble by old age.

come wandering up to the house and meet the lion; but she would be needing to be milked, come six or seven o'clock, and that got to worrying May. She also worried how long a sick mountain lion might hang around, keeping her shut in the house. May didn't like being shut in.

"I went out a time or two, and went shoo!"

Eyes shining amidst fine wrinkles, she flaps her thin arms at the lion. "Shoo! Go on home now!"

But the silent wild creature watches her with yellow eyes and does not stir.

"So when I was talking to Miss Macy on the telephone, she said it might have rabies, and I ought to call the sheriff. I was uneasy then. So finally I did that, and they come out, those county police, you know. Two carloads."

Her voice is dry and quiet.

"I guess there was nothing else they knew how to do. So they shot it."

She looks off across the field Old Jim, her brother, used to plow with Prince the horse and irrigate with the water from this tank. Now wild oats and blackberry grow there. In another thirty years it will be a rich man's vineyard, a tax write-off.

"He was seven feet long, all stretched out, before they took him off. And so thin! They all said, 'Well, Aunt May, I guess you were scared there! I guess you were some scared!' But I wasn't. I didn't want him shot. But I didn't know what to do for him. And I did need to get to Rosie."

I have told this true story which May gave to us as truly as I could, and now I want to tell it as fiction, yet without taking it from her: rather to give it back to her, if I can do so. It is a tiny part of the history of the Valley, and I want to make it part of the Valley outside history. Now the field that the poor man plowed and the rich man harvested lies on the edge of a little town, houses and workshops of timber and fieldstone standing among almond, oak, and eucalyptus trees; and now May is an old woman with a name that means the month of May: Rains End. An old woman with a long, wrinkled-pleated upper lip, she is living alone for the summer in her summer place, a meadow a mile or so up in the hills above the little town. Sinshan. She took her cow Rose with her, and since Rose tends to wander she keeps her on a long tether[10] down by the tiny creek, and moves her into fresh grass now and then. The summer-house is what they call a nine-pole house, a mere frame of poles stuck in the ground—one of them is a live digger-pine sapling—with stick and matting walls, and mat roof and floors. It doesn't rain in the dry season, and the roof is just for shade. But the house and its little front yard where Rains End has her camp stove and clay oven and matting loom are well shaded by a fig tree that was planted there a hundred years or so ago by her grandmother.

Rains End herself has no grandchildren; she never bore a child, and her one or two marriages were brief and very long ago. She has a nephew and two grand-nieces, and feels herself an aunt to all children, even when they are afraid of her and rude to her because she has got so ugly with old age, smelling as musty as a chickenhouse. She considers it natural for children to shrink away from somebody part way dead, and knows that when they're a little older and have got used to her they'll ask her for stories. She was for sixty years a member of the Doctors Lodge, and though she doesn't do curing any more people still ask her to help with nursing sick children, and the children come to long for the kind, authoritative touch of her hands when she bathes them to bring a fever down, or changes a dressing, or combs out bed-tangled hair with witch hazel[11] and great patience.

---

[10] tether—rope or chain used to keep an animal confined within certain limits.

[11] witch hazel—a soothing and mildly astringent lotion.

So Rains End was just waking up from an early afternoon nap in the heat of the day, under the matting roof, when she heard a noise, a huge, awful yowl that started soft with a nasal hum and rose slowly into a snarling gargle that sank away into a sobbing purr. . . . And she got up and looked out from the open side of the house of sticks and matting, and saw a mountain lion under the fig tree. She looked at him from her house; he looked at her from his.

And this part of the story is much the same: the old woman; the lion; and, down by the creek, the cow.

It was hot. Crickets sang shrill in the yellow grass on all the hills and canyons, in all the chaparral.[12] Rains End filled a bowl with water from an unglazed jug and came slowly out of the house. Halfway between the house and the lion she set the bowl down on the dirt. She turned and went back to the house.

The lion got up after a while and came and sniffed at the water. He lay down again with a soft, **querulous**[9] groan, almost like a sick child, and looked at Rains End with the yellow eyes that saw her in a different way than she had ever been seen before.

She sat on the matting in the shade of the open part of her house and did some mending. When she looked up at the lion she sang under her breath, tunelessly; she wanted to remember the Puma Dance Song but could only remember bits of it, so she made a song for the occasion:

You are there, lion.
You are there, lion. . . .

As the afternoon wore on she began to worry about going down to milk Rose. Unmilked, the cow would

---

[12] chaparral—dense thicket of shrubs.

[13] **querulous**—whining.

start tugging at her tether and making a commotion. That was likely to upset the lion. He lay so close to the house now that if she came out that too might upset him, and she did not want to frighten him or to become frightened of him. He had evidently come for some reason, and it behoved[14] her to find out what the reason was. Probably he was sick; his coming so close to a human person was strange, and people who behave strangely are usually sick or in some kind of pain. Sometimes, though, they are spiritually moved to act strangely. The lion might be a messenger, or might have some message of his own for her or her townspeople. She was more used to seeing birds as messengers; the four-footed people go about their own business. But the lion, dweller in the Seventh House,[15] comes from the place dreams come from. Maybe she did not understand. Maybe someone else would understand. She could go over and tell Valiant and her family, whose summerhouse was in Gahheya meadow, farther up the creek; or she could go over to Buck's, on Baldy Knoll. But there were four or five adolescents there, and one of them might come and shoot the lion, to boast that he'd saved old Rains End from getting clawed to bits and eaten.

Mooooooo! said Rose, down by the creek, reproachfully.

The sun was still above the southwest ridge, but the branches of pines were across it and the heavy heat was out of it, and shadows were welling up in the low fields of wild oats and blackberry.

Moooooo! said Rose again, louder.

The lion lifted up his square, heavy head, the color of dry wild oats, and gazed down across the pastures. Rains End knew from that weary movement that he

---

[14] behoved—was fitting or proper for.

[15] Seventh House—refers to the houses of the zodiac. The Seventh House governs relationships and unions.

was very ill. He had come for company in dying, that was all.

"I'll come back, lion," Rains End sang tunelessly. "Lie still. Be quiet. I'll come back soon." Moving softly and easily, as she would move in a room with a sick child, she got her milking pail and stool, slung the stool on her back with a woven strap so as to leave a hand free, and came out of the house. The lion watched her at first very tense, the yellow eyes firing up for a moment, but then put his head down again with that little grudging, groaning sound. "I'll come back, lion," Rains End said. She went down to the creekside and milked a nervous and indignant cow. Rose could smell lion, and demanded in several ways, all **eloquent**,[16] just what Rains End intended to *do*? Rains End ignored her questions and sang milking songs to her: "Su bonny, su bonny, be still my grand cow. . ." Once she had to slap her hard on the hip. "Quit that, you old fool! Get over! I am *not* going to untie you and have you walking into trouble! I won't let him come down this way."

She did not say how she planned to stop him.

She retethered[17] Rose where she could stand down in the creek if she liked. When she came back up the rise with the pail of milk in hand, the lion had not moved. The sun was down, the air above the ridges turning clear gold. The yellow eyes watched her, no light in them. She came to pour the milk into the lion's bowl. As she did so, he all at once half rose up. Rains End started, and spilled some of the milk she was pouring. "Shoo! Stop that!" she whispered fiercely, waving her skinny arm at the lion. "Lie down now! I'm afraid of you when you get up, can't you see that, stupid? Lie down now, lion. There you are. Here I am. It's all right. You know what you're doing." Talking softly as she

---

[16] **eloquent**—expressive, effective, and stirring.

[17] retethered—tied again.

went, she returned to her house of stick and matting. There she sat down as before, in the open porch, on the grass mats.

The mountain lion made the grumbling sound, ending with a long sigh, and let his head sink back down on his paws.

Rains End got some cornbread and a tomato from the pantry box while there was still daylight left to see by, and ate slowly and neatly. She did not offer the lion food. He had not touched the milk, and she thought he would eat no more in the House of Earth.

From time to time as the quiet evening darkened and stars gathered thicker overhead she sang to the lion. She sang the five songs of *Going Westward to the Sunrise*, which are sung to human beings dying. She did not know if it was proper and appropriate to sing these songs to a dying mountain lion, but she did not know his songs.

Twice he also sang: once a **quavering**[18] moan, like a house cat challenging another torn to battle, and once a long, sighing purr.

Before the Scorpion[19] had swung clear of Sinshan Mountain, Rains End had pulled her heavy shawl around herself in case the fog came in, and had gone sound asleep in the porch of her house.

She woke with the grey light before sunrise. The lion was a motionless shadow, a little farther from the trunk of the fig tree than he had been the night before. As the light grew, she saw that he had stretched himself out full length. She knew he had finished his dying, and sang the fifth song, the last song, in a whisper, for him:

The doors of the Four Houses
are open.
Surely they are open.

---

[18] **quavering**—trembling.

[19] Scorpion—a scorpion-shaped constellation, or configuration of stars, in the skies of the Southern Hemisphere.

Near sunrise she went to milk Rose, and to wash in the creek. When she came back up to the house she went closer to the lion, though not so close as to crowd him, and stood for a long time looking at him stretched out in the long, **tawny**,[20] delicate light. "As thin as I am!" she said to Valiant, when she went up to Gahheya later in the morning to tell the story and to ask help carrying the body of the lion off where the buzzards and coyotes could clean it.

It's still your story, Aunt May; it was your lion. He came to you. He brought his death to you, a gift; but the men with the guns won't take gifts, they think they own death already. And so they took from you the honor he did you, and you felt that loss. I wanted to restore it. But you don't need it. You followed the lion where he went, years ago now.

---

[20] **tawny**—warm, brownish-orange colored.

QUESTIONS TO CONSIDER

1. Who narrates this account of May and the lion? In what way did the narrator liberate May's voice in the retelling of her story?

2. Why do you think the narrator felt the need to retell May's story?

3. What cultural elements are added in the retelling, and why? Why is May renamed "Rains End"? What does this name change about May herself?

4. What is the significance of the two very different endings to May's story? What is given back to May in the retelling that was taken from her in her version of the story?

All Living as Repeating

BY GERTRUDE STEIN

Gertrude Stein (1874–1946) was was one of America's most gifted experimental writers. She sought to liberate language from the bondage of rules devised by men in order to communicate the feelings behind words in new, expressive ways. Her unique way of using language inspired many other writers, including Ernest Hemingway and F. Scott Fitzgerald, and she is known today as much for her influence on the writing of others as she is for her own. Her most well-known work is The Autobiography of Alice B. Toklas, *in which Stein writes about herself through the eyes and pen of her friend. The following excerpt is from her long prose work* The Making of Americans *(written 1906–1908, published in 1925). This work is the story of a fictional character, Martha Hersland, who represents Stein and her family. Stein's characteristic use of simple words and repetition can be seen here.*

Always from the beginning there was to me all living as repeating. This is now a description of my feeling. As I was saying listening to repeating is often irritating,[1] always repeating is all of living, everything in a being is always repeating, more and more listening to repeating gives to me completed understanding. Each one slowly comes to be a whole one to me. Each one slowly comes to be a whole one in me. Soon then it commences to sound through my ears and eyes and feelings the repeating that is always coming out from each one, that is them, that makes then slowly of each one of them a whole one. Repeating then comes slowly then to be to one who has it to have loving repeating as natural being comes to be a full sound telling all the being in each one such a one is ever knowing. Sometimes it takes many years of knowing some one before the repeating that is that one gets to be a steady sounding to the hearing of one who has it as a natural being to love repeating that slowly comes out from every one. Sometimes it takes many years of knowing some one before the repeating in that one comes to be a clear history of such a one. Natures sometimes are so mixed up in some one that steady repeating in them is mixed up with changing. Soon then there will be a completed history of each one. Sometimes it is difficult to know it in some, for what these are saying is repeating in them is not the real repeating of them, is not the complete repeating for them. Sometimes many years of knowing some one pass before repeating of all being in them comes out clearly from them. As I was saying it is often irritating to listen to the repeating

[1] Stein is admitting that her technique may be irritating to the reader, but she is pointing out that life and people are repetitive, and that too can be irritating.

they are doing, always then that one that has it as being to love repeating that is the whole history of each one, such a one has it then that this irritation passes over into patient completed understanding. Loving repeating is one way of being. This is now a description of such feeling.[2]

There are many that I know and they know it. They are all of them repeating and I hear it. I love it and I tell it. I love it and now I will write it. This is now a history of my love of it. I hear it and I love it and I write it. They repeat it. They live it and I see it and I hear it. They live it and I hear it and I see it and I love it and now and always I will write it. There are many kinds of men and women and I know it. They repeat it and I hear it and I love it. This is now a history of the way they do it. This is now a history of the way I love it.[3]

---

[2] These three sentences are the heart of the passage. Irritation with a person passes to understanding and love. Her writing is describing it.

[3] By telling people's story (their history) with such care, Stein is showing her love for them and the story is about both their lives and her love.

QUESTIONS TO CONSIDER

1. What is the theme of Stein's writing?

2. Why does Stein feel that although it can be irritating, repeating is valuable?

3. What small changes do you find each time Stein repeats an idea? What do the changes add to the overall meaning of what she is saying?

4. Why, according to Stein, is it important to know a person over a long period of time?

5. What do you think Stein considers to be the role, or roles, of a writer in relation to life?

6. In what ways can Stein be considered a liberating voice in the world of women's writing?

▲

Asserting Their Demands A group of strong-minded women demand the opportunity to vote at a New York polling place in 1875. As voting was still illegal at the time, they only succeeded in creating a commotion.

▲

The Women's Suffrage Amendment First introduced in
1878, the 19th Amendment, which gave women the right to vote,
wasn't ratified until 1920. Here three women stand outside the
Suffrage League Building.

Early Protests A group of suffragists picket outside a jail
to protest the imprisonment of women arrested during
their protests. ▶

THE SUFFRAGE PRISONERS
WERE ARRESTED FOR A
POLITICAL OFFENSE.
WE DEMAND
THAT THEY BE TREATED AS
POLITICAL OFFENDERS.

Laborers During World War II (1939–1945) millions of women worked in factories and in other labor-intensive jobs to aid the war effort. Some, like the women shown here, worked in railroad yards.

Morale Posters like this one depicted strong women making sacrifices for the common good. ▶

We Can Do I

▲

Commitment Two women wear oxygen masks to protect themselves from hazardous gases in a munitions plant.

▲

When the war ended in 1945, returning soldiers reentered the work force.
Women were encouraged to give up their work, become full-time housewives,
and devote themselves to their families. This family of four represents the ideal
image of the 1950s.

Two Views of Housework On the one hand, a bored and weary housewife dutifully irons her husband's shirt while he is away at work. On the other, the stereotyped 1950s housewife, cheerfully vacuums. Images like this caused many women to wonder why *they* didn't feel like smiling when *they* did housework, and even more, why they felt unfulfilled and mentally unchallenged.

Equal Rights The drive for equal rights gained momentum in the 1960s. With the support of the National Organization for Women and other feminist groups, women lobbied for rights and opportunities they had so long been denied in the areas of employment, education, and reproductive rights. At a Women's Liberation march in New York City, a group of women hold posters expressing their demands.

▲

Sit-in Members of NOW chain themselves to the White House fence to protest President Reagan's opposition to the Equal Rights Amendment, a proposed addition to the Constitution guaranteeing that "Equality of rights under the law shall not be denied or abridged by the United States or by any state on account of sex." The ERA was defeated in 1982, when, faced with fierce opposition, it failed to gain the necessary approval for ratification.

Pro-Choice/Pro-Life One of the most controversial issues in the women's movement is the idea that a woman's right to control over her own body means control of her right to choose an abortion. Women themselves are split on this issue.

▲

Victory The U.S. Women's Soccer team's victory at the 1999 World Cup competition was not only a triumph for the nation, but also for women around the world. At no other time in history had women been more recognized and celebrated for their mental strength and physical power.

▲

Soaring to New Heights Astronaut Sally Ride arrives at the Kennedy Space Center in Cape Canaveral, Florida in 1983. She endured a rigorous selection process to become the first American woman to go to space.

▲

The prestigious Nobel Prize for Literature is awarded every year to an author who has written particularly distinguished material. Nadine Gordimer (left) and Toni Morrison (right) won Nobels in 1991 and 1993, respectively. Their work continues to earn wide acclaim from critics and readers alike.

Defining Me

Vive Noir!

BY MARI EVANS

Born in Toledo, Ohio, Mari Evans studied fashion design before she decided to become a full-time writer. Although best known for her poetry, she has written short stories, plays, and has produced an anthology of African-American literary criticism. Evans began writing poetry as a result of the encouragement of her father and of her interest in the work of Harlem Renaissance poet Langston Hughes. Her first volume of poetry, Where Is All the Music?, *was published in 1968. The rhythm and beat of her poetry reflect the political urgency and optimism felt by African Americans during the Civil Rights movement of the 1960s. "Vive Noir!" celebrates a vision of positive black identity and empowerment.[1]*

i
am going to rise
en masse[2]
from Inner City

---

[1] The poem's title, "Vive Noir!" means "Long Live Black!" in French.

[2] en masse—in mass, in a body (French).

                    sick
                        of newyork ghettos
                        chicago tenements
                        l a's slums
weary
            of exhausted lands
            sagging **privies**[3]
            saying yessuh yessuh
            yesSIR
            in an assortment
            of geographical **dialects**[4] i
have seen my last
broken down plantation
even from a
distance
                        i
will load all my goods
in '50 Chevy pickups '53
Fords fly United and '66
caddys i
            have packed in
            the old man and the old lady and
            wiped the children's noses
            I'm tired
              of hand me downs
                shut me ups
                  pin me ups
                    keep me outs
                      messing me over have
                    just had it
                  baby
                from
                you . . .

---

[3] **privies**—outhouses.

[4] **dialects**—regional varieties of languages distinguished by different grammar, vocabulary, or pronunciation.

i'm
gonna spread out
over America
                intrude
my proud blackness
all
        over the place
                i have **wrested**[5] wheat fields
                from the forests

                turned rivers
                from their courses

                leveled mountains
                at a word
                festooned the land with
                bridges
                    gemlike
                    on **filaments**[6] of steel
                        moved
            glistening towersofBabel[7] in place
                like blocks
            sweated a whole
            civilization
                . . . for you
            now
                    i'm
            gonna breathe fire
            through flaming nostrils BURN
                a place for
                    me
        in the skyscrapers and the
        schoolrooms on the green

---

[5] **wrested**—pulled or twisted forcefully.

[6] **filaments**—thin threads of steel wire.

[7] towersofBabel—reference to the construction of a building in the biblical city of Babylon, whose construction ended when the builders became unable to understand each other.

lawns and the white
beaches
          i'm
gonna wear the robes and
sit on the benches
make the rules and make
the arrests say
who can and who
can't
          baby you don't stand
          a
          chance
i'm

gonna put black angels
in all the books and a black
Christchild in Mary's arms i'm
gonna make black bunnies black
fairies black santas black
nursery rhymes and
                    black
ice cream
               i'm
gonna make it a
     crime
          to be anything BUT black
          pass the coppertone[8]

---

[8] coppertone—a reference to suntan lotion. A humorous suggestion on how
white people can get some color!

QUESTIONS TO CONSIDER

1. What is the speaker's message to the black community?

2. Who else is the speaker addressing in this poem?

3. What is the tone and feeling of this poem?

Ancestors: In Praise of the Imperishable

BY SANDRA JACKSON-OPOKU

Poet, novelist, and travel journalist Sandra Jackson-Opoku became interested in her African heritage in 1974 when she was an exchange student in Nigeria. Born and raised in Chicago, Jackson-Opoku has received numerous awards for her writing, including the National Endowment for the Arts Fellowship and the General Electric Foundation Award for young writers. The following poem calls forth the importance and timeless endurance of African ancestors who serve as an important life force for African Americans.

Much more than just one woman,
there are endless spirits
roaming inside me
River Mothers
moving, and
memory much
older
I
And
who but we
fall heir to such
memory, such dream?

River Mothers moving,
History wrapped around my tongue

There are spirits, stirring inside me

QUESTIONS TO CONSIDER

1. Who are the River Mothers that Jackson-Opoku refers to? What does she mean by "History wrapped around my tongue"?

2. What meaning does the visual structure and overall "look" of the printed poem on the page convey? How does it add to the message the poet wishes to communicate?

3. What does Jackson-Opoku want to give her readers through her poem that she experienced herself?

4. Does your history have to be all "good" to be helpful to you? How do you think Jackson-Opoku would answer the question? How would you answer it for yourself?

from

Heartburn

BY NORA EPHRON

Although best known for her work as a screenwriter and movie director, Nora Ephron (1941–   ) began her career writing humor and satire. Ephron won an Oscar nomination for her screenplay for the movie Silkwood *in 1986. She also received wide acclaim for writing and directing* Sleepless in Seattle *in 1993. The following selection is excerpted from Ephron's first novel,* Heartburn, *the story of Rachel Samstat, whose marriage to Mark is breaking up while she is seven months pregnant with their second child. The title of this humorous work is a pun recalling the indigestion that accompanies pregnancy and the heartache of divorce. In this excerpt, Rachel reminisces about her career in writing about food.*

Obviously I didn't start out in life wanting to be a food writer. These days there are probably people who do—just as there are now people who start out wanting to be film critics, God help us—but I started out wanting to be a journalist. Which I became. I was a reporter for the *New York World-Telegram and Sun* and I lived in a junior two-and-a-half, and whenever I was home alone at night I cooked myself a perfect little dinner. None of your containers of yogurt for me; no, sir. I would pick a recipe from Michael Field or Julia Child[1] and shop on the way home and spend the first part of the evening painstakingly mastering whatever dish I had chosen. Then I would sit down to eat it in front of the television set. At the time I thought this was wildly civilized behavior, but the truth is it was probably somewhat Mamie Eisenhowerish.[2] In any case, I learned to cook. Everyone did—everyone my age, that is. This was the mid-1960s, the height of the first wave of competitive cooking. I'm always interested when people talk about the sixties in the kind of hushed tone that is meant to **connote**[3] the seriousness of it all, because what I remember about the sixties was that people were constantly looking up from dessert and saying things like: "Whose mousse[4] is this?" Once, I remember, one of my friends called up to say his marriage had ended on account of veal Orloff, and I knew exactly what he meant. It was quite mad, really. I was never completely idiotic—I never once made a quiche,[5] for example—but I held my own, and I'm afraid that I'm still known in certain circles as the originator of a game called If You Had to Have Only One Flavor Soufflé for the Rest of Your Life, Would It Be Chocolate or Grand Marnier?

Anyway, there I was at the *World-Telegram* when the food editor retired. There was a pause before the next food editor arrived, and I was asked to fill in and write the "A Visit With" column. You know the kind of column it was: I would go to interview famous people in their homes, and they'd talk about their dinner parties and their decorators and their **indispensable**[6] housekeepers,

---

[1] Michael Field and Julia Child are authors of recipes for fine dining.

[2] Mamie Eisenhower (1896–1979) was the wife of former President Dwight D. Eisenhower. She was not a stylish woman.

[3] **connote**—suggest or imply.

[4] mousse—a light, frothy dish.

[5] quiche—main course pie made of eggs and cheese.

[6] **indispensable**—essential, necessary.

and then, in the end, they'd give me a recipe. The recipes weren't much—you'd be amazed at how many legendary hostesses tried to get away with newlywed garbage like chicken Divan and grapes with sour cream and brown sugar—but the interviews were really quite fascinating. People would say the oddest things about the servant problem and the extra-man-at-the-dinner-party problem and tipping at Christmas and how you could tell the economy was getting worse because of all the chicken you were starting to see at dinner parties. "Dark-meat chicken," one woman said to me **contemptuously**.[7]

It was just a mild little column in a newspaper no one read, but as a result of it, I began to have a field of expertise. That's probably putting it too strongly—it wasn't as if I had become an expert in law or economics or seventeenth-century England—but that's how it felt: having spent my life knowing nothing much about anything (which is known as being a generalist), I suddenly knew something about something. I certainly knew enough to make jokes in the food-world language. I learned that the words "monosodium glutamate"[8] were almost automatically funny, especially aloud, as were "The R. T. French's Mustard Tastemaker Award," "The Pillsbury Bake-Off" and "The National Chicken Cooking Contest." This gave me an edge as a food writer that almost made up for the fact that I think that certain serious food-world subjects, like coulibiac[9] of salmon (another automatically funny phrase), are not worth bothering with.

(Another argument I have with serious food people is that they're always talking about how *creative* cooking is. "Cooking is very creative" is how they put it. Now, there's no question that there are a handful of people doing genuinely creative things with food—although a lot of it, if you ask me, seems to consist of heating up

---

[7] **contemptuously**—with disrespect.

[8] monosodium glutamate—a crystalline salt used in seasoning.

[9] coulibiac—fish pie.

goat cheese or throwing strawberry vinegar onto calves' liver or relying excessively on the kiwi. But most cooking is based on elementary, long-standing principles, and to say that cooking is creative not only misses the point of creativity—which is that it is painful and difficult and quite unrelated to whether it is possible to come up with yet another way to cook a pork chop—but also misses the whole point of cooking, which is that it is totally mindless. What I love about cooking is that after a hard day, there is something comforting about the fact that if you melt butter and add flour and then hot stock, *it will get thick!* It's a sure thing! It's a sure thing in a world where nothing is sure; it has a mathematical certainty in a world where those of us who long for some kind of certainty are forced to settle for crossword puzzles.)

Normally I enjoy doing food demonstrations—I like giving my speech, I like the way it laces in and out of the subject of food. But when I was about halfway through the demonstration at Macy's—I was right in the middle of cooking Lillian Hellman's[10] pot roast—I realized I was in trouble. Lillian Hellman's pot roast is the sort of recipe that makes my reputation in the food world what it is, since it contains all sorts of low-rent ingredients like a package of onion soup mix and a can of cream of mushroom soup. It even has something called Kitchen Bouquet in it, although I always leave it out. You take a nice 4-pound piece of beef, the more expensive the better, and put it into a good pot with 1 can of cream of mushroom soup, an envelope of dried onion soup, 1 large chopped onion, 3 cloves chopped garlic, 2 cups red wine and 2 cups water. Add a crushed bay leaf and 1 teaspoon each thyme and basil. Cover and bake in a 350° oven until tender, 3 1/2 hours or so.

It's a small point, just an aside that gets me through measuring the liquid ingredients, but it occurred to me

---

[10] Lillian Hellman (1905–1984) was a major playwright of the mid-twentieth century who lived in New York City.

as I delivered it yet another time that I had always zipped through that part of the speech as if I had somehow managed to be invulnerable to the fantasy, as if I had somehow managed to escape from or rise above it simply as a result of having figured it out. I think you often have that sense when you write—that if you can spot something in yourself and set it down on paper, you're free of it. And you're not, of course; you've just managed to set it down on paper, that's all. The truth is that I'm at least as big a sap about romance as old Lillian was, probably even bigger.

I'll give you another example. I've written about cooking and marriage dozens of times, and I'm very smart on the subject, I'm very smart about how complicated things get when food and love become hopelessly tangled. But I realized as I stood there doing my demonstration in the middle of the Macy's housewares department that I had been as dopey about food and love as any old-fashioned Jewish mother. I loved to cook, so I cooked. And then the cooking became a way of saying I love you. And then the cooking became the easy way of saying I love you. And then the cooking became the only way of saying I love you. I was so busy perfecting the peach pie that I wasn't paying attention. I had never even been able to imagine an alternative. Every so often I would look at my women friends who were happily married and didn't cook, and I would always find myself wondering how they did it. Would anyone love me if I couldn't cook? I always thought cooking was part of the package: Step right up, it's Rachel Samstat, she's bright, she's funny, *and she can cook!*

QUESTIONS TO CONSIDER

1. What is heartburn? Why do you think that Ephron chose *Heartburn* as the title for her novel?

2. Historically, what has been Rachel's relationship with food? Why is food so important to her?

3. What is the tone of Rachel's writing? What role does writing serve for Rachel in a time of personal crisis?

4. How has Rachel defined herself alone and as part of a relationship? What has caused her to question her old idea of who she is?

5. What is the meaning of the last line "I always thought cooking was part of the package: Step right up, it's Rachel Samstat, she's bright, she's funny, *and she can cook!*"? How could you rewrite this sentence to reflect what Rachel is learning about herself?

The Mulatto Millennium

BY DANZY SENNA

Danzy Senna was born in 1970 in Boston, Massachusetts. Senna has worked as a journalist for Newsweek *and* SPIN *and is the author of the novel* Caucasia. *The daughter of a white mother and black-Mexican father, Senna brings to her writing rich insights about being of mixed parentage in a country obsessed with racial identification. "The Mulatto Millenium" is from* Half and Half: Writers on Growing Up Biracial and Bicultural *(1998), edited by Claudine O'Hearn. In it, Senna discusses the identity questions she confronted in growing up.*

Strange to wake up and realize you're in style. That's what happened to me just the other morning. It was the first day of the new millennium and I woke to find that mulattos[1] had taken over. They were everywhere. Playing golf, running the airwaves, opening their own restaurants, modeling clothes, starring in musicals with

---

[1] mulattos—persons of mixed race.

names like *Show Me the **Miscegenation**!*[2] The radio played a steady stream of Lenny Kravitz, Sade, and Mariah Carey. I thought I'd died and gone to Berkeley. But then I realized. According to the racial zodiac, 2000 is the official Year of the Mulatto. Pure breeds (at least the black ones) are out and **hybridity**[3] is in. America loves us in all of our half-caste glory. The president announced on Friday that beige is to be the official color of the millennium. Major news magazines announce our arrival as if we were proof of extraterrestrial life. They claim we're going to bring about the end of race as we know it.

It has been building for a while, this mulatto fever. But it was this morning that it really reached its peak. I awoke early to a loud ruckus outside—horns and drums and flutes playing "Kum ba Yah"[4] outside my window. I went to the porch to witness a mass of **bedraggled**[5] activists making their way down Main Street. They were chanting, not quite in unison, "Mulattos Unite, Take Back the White!" I had a hard time making out the placards through the tangle of dreadlocks[6] and loose Afros. At the front of the crowd, two brown-skinned women in Birkenstocks[7] carried a banner that read FOR COLORED GIRLS WHO HAVE CONSIDERED JEW BOYS WHEN THE NEGROES AIN'T ENOUGH. A lean yellow girl with her hair in messy Afro-puffs wore a T-shirt with the words JUST HUMAN across the front. What appeared to be a Hasidic Jew walked hand in hand with his girlfriend, a Japanese woman in traditional attire, the two of them wearing huge yellow buttons on their lapels that read MAKE MULATTOS, NOT WAR. I trailed

---

[2] *Miscegenation*—a negative term for sexual relations or marriage between people of different races.

[3] **hybridity**—mixed origin.

[4] Kum ba Yah—a folk song that was popular during the 1960s.

[5] **bedraggled**—soiled; stained; deteriorated.

[6] dreadlocks—braided strands of hair.

[7] Birkenstocks—loose-fitting, sandal-like shoes first created in Germany.

behind the parade for some miles, not quite sure I wanted to join or stay at the heels of this group.

I guess I should have seen it coming. Way back in the fall of 1993, *Time* magazine put on its cover "The New Face of America," a computer-morphed face of fourteen models of different racial backgrounds, creating a woman they named Eve. The managing editor wrote:

> The woman on the cover of this special issue of *Time* does not exist except metaphysically. . . . The highlight of this exercise in cybergenesis[8] was the creation of the woman on our cover, selected as a symbol of the future, multiethnic face of America. . . . As onlookers watched the image of our new Eve begin to appear on the computer screen, several staff members promptly fell in love. Said one: "It really breaks my heart that she doesn't exist." We sympathize with our lovelorn colleagues, but even technology has its limits. This is a love that must forever remain unrequited.

Of course, anyone could see that women just like the computer face they had created did exist in Puerto Rico, Latin America, and Spanish Harlem. But the editors at *Time* remained unaware of this, seeming to prefer their colored folk imaginary, not real. As I read the article, it reminded me of an old saying they used to have down South during Jim Crow:[9] "If a black man wants to sit at the front of the bus, he just puts on a turban." Maybe the same rule applied here: call yourself mixed and you just might find the world smiles a little brighter on you.

Mulattos may not be new. But the mulatto-pride folks are a new generation. They want their own special

---

[8] cybergenesis—computer creation.

[9] Jim Crow—the time of systematic practice of discrimination and suppression against black people in the United States.

category or no categories at all. They're a full-fledged movement, complete with their own share of extremists. As I wandered at the edges of the march this morning, one woman gave me a flyer. It was a **treatise**[10] on biracial superiority, which began, "Ever wonder why mutts are always smarter than full-breed dogs?" The rest of her treatise was dense and incomprehensible: something about the sun people and the ice people coming together to create the perfectly **temperate**[11] being. Another man, a militant dressed like Huey P. Newton,[12] came toward me waving a rifle in his hand. He told me that those who refuse to miscegenate should be shot. I steered clear of him, instead burying my head in a newspaper. I opened to the book review section, and at the top of the best-seller list were three memoirs: *Kimchee and Grits,* by Kyong Washington, *Gefilte Fish and Ham Hocks,* by Schlomo Jackson, and at the top of the list, and for the third week in a row, *Burritos and Borsht,* by a cat named Julio Werner. That was it. In a fit of nausea, I took off running for home.

Before all of this radical **ambiguity**,[13] I was a black girl. I fear even saying this. The political strong arm of the multiracial movement, affectionately known as the Mulatto Nation (just "the M.N." for those in the know), decreed just yesterday that those who refuse to comply with orders to embrace their many heritages will be sent on the first plane to Rio de Janeiro, Brazil, where, the M.N.'s minister of defense said, "they might learn the true meaning of mestizo[14] power."

But, with all due respect to the multiracial movement, I cannot tell a lie. I was a black girl. Not your ordinary black girl, if such a thing exists. But rather, a black girl with a Wasp mother and a black-Mexican

---

[10] **treatise**—formal written statement on a subject.

[11] **temperate**—moderate, middle-of-the-road.

[12] Huey P. Newton—one of the founders of the Black Panther Party, an African-American militant organization founded in the 1960s.

[13] **ambiguity**—uncertainty, obscurity.

[14] mestizo—referring to persons of European and Native American ancestry.

father, and a face that harkens to Andalusia,[15] not Africa. I was born in 1970, when "black" described a people bonded not by shared complexion or hair texture but by shared history.

Not only was I black (and here I go out on a limb), but I was an enemy of the people. The mulatto people, that is. I sneered at those byproducts of miscegenation who chose to identify as mixed, not black. I thought it wishy-washy, an act of **flagrant assimilation**,[16] treason, passing even.

It was my parents who made me this way. In Boston **circa**[17] 1975, mixed wasn't really an option. You were either white or black. No checking "Other." No halvsies. No in-between. Black people, being the bottom of the social totem pole in Boston, were inevitably the most accepting of difference; they were the only race to come in all colors, and so there I found myself. Sure, I received some strange reactions from all quarters when I called myself black. But black people usually got over their initial surprise and welcomed me into the ranks. It was white folks who grew the most uncomfortable with the **dissonance**[18] between the face they saw and the race they didn't. Upon learning who I was, they grew paralyzed with fear that they might have "slipped up" in my presence, that is, said something racist, not knowing there was a Negro in their midst. Often, they had.

Let it be clear—my parents' decision to raise us as black wasn't based on any one-drop rule from the days of slavery, and it certainly wasn't based on our appearance, that crude reasoning many black-identified mixed people use: if the world sees me as black, I must be black. If it had been based on appearance, my sister

---

[15] Andalusia—a region of southern Spain on the Mediterranean Sea.

[16] **flagrant assimilation**—scandalous absorption into another culture.

[17] **circa**—(Latin) around; about.

[18] **dissonance**—conflict; disagreement.

would have been black, my brother Mexican, and me Jewish. Instead, my parents' decision arose out of the rising black power movement, which made identifying as black not a pseudoscientific rule but a conscious choice. *You told us all along that we had to call ourselves black because of this so-called one drop. Now that we don't have to anymore, we choose to. Because black is beautiful. Because black is not a burden, but a privilege.*

Some might say my parents went too far in their struggle to instill a black identity in us. I remember my father schooling me and my siblings on our racial identity. He would hold his own version of the Inquisition,[19] grilling us over a greasy linoleum kitchen table while a single, bright lightbulb swung overhead. He would ask: "Do you have any black friends?" "How many?" "Who?" "What are their names?" And we, his obedient children, his soldiers in the battle for **negritude**,[20] would rattle off the names of the black kids we called friends. (When we, trying to turn the tables, asked my father why all his girlfriends were white, he would launch into one of his famously circular **diatribes**,[21] which left us spinning with confusion. I only remember that his reasoning involved demographics and the slim chances of him meeting a black woman in the Brookline Public Library on a Monday afternoon.)

But something must have sunk in, because my sister and I grew up with a disdain for those who identified as mulatto rather than black. Not all mulattos bothered me back then. It was a very particular breed that got under my skin: the kind who answered, meekly, "Everything," to that incessant question "What are you?" Populist author Jim Hightower wrote a book called *There's*

---

[19] Inquisition—former effort by the Roman Catholic Church to find and punish those who opposed the Church's teachings through intense examination and questioning.

[20] **negritude**—taking pride in being black.

[21] **diatribes**—bitter lectures or arguments.

Nothing in the Middle of the Road but Yellow Stripes and Dead Armadillos. That's what mulattos represented to me back then: yellow stripes and dead armadillos. Something to be avoided. I veered away from groups of them—children, like myself, who had been born of interracial minglings after dark. Instead, I surrounded myself with bodies darker than myself, hoping the color might rub off on me.

I used to spy on white people, blend into their crowd, let them think I was one of them, and then listen as they talked in smug disdain about black folks. It wasn't something I had to search out. And most white people, I found, no matter how much they preach MLK's[22] dream, are just as obsessed with color and difference as the rest of us. They just talk about it in more coded terms. Around white folks, I never had to bring up race. They brought it up for me, and I listened, my skin tingling slightly, my stomach twisting in anger, as they revealed their true feelings about colored folks. Then I would spring it on them, tell them who I really was, and watch, in a kind of pained glee, as their faces went from eggshell white, to rose pink, to hot mama crimson, to The Color Purple.[23] Afterward, I would report back to headquarters, where my friends would laugh and holler about how I was an undercover Negro.

There had been moments in my life when I had not asserted my black identity. I hadn't "passed" in the traditional sense of the word, but in a more subtle way, by simply mumbling that I was mixed. Then the white people in my midst seemed to forget whom they were talking to, and countless times I was a silent witness to their candid racism. When I would remind them that my father was black, they would laugh and say, "But you're

---

[22] MLK's—Martin Luther King, Jr.'s.

[23] The Color Purple—refers to Alice Walker's Pulitzer Prize-winning novel of the struggles of an impoverished and abused African-American woman.

different." That was somewhere I never wanted to return. There was danger in this muddy middle stance. A danger of disappearing. Of being swallowed whole by the great white whale. I had seen the arctic belly of the beast and didn't plan on returning.

QUESTIONS TO CONSIDER

1. Why does Senna begin with a fantasy for the new millenium? What is the point of the picture she paints in the beginning?

2. What did being neither 100 percent black nor white mean to Senna when she was growing up? What difficulties did she face?

3. Why did Senna's parents want to raise their children with a strong black identity?

4. What do you think Senna has learned about her own identity? Do you think she would raise her own children in a different way from the way she was raised? Why or why not?

Living Like Weasels

BY ANNIE DILLARD

Annie Dillard (1945–   ) won a Pulitzer Prize at the age of 30 for her first novel, Pilgrim at Tinker Creek. *Since then she has written an autobiography, three novels, and several collections of poetry and essays. In much of her writing she explores the spiritual relationship between humankind and nature. In the following essay from her book,* Teaching a Stone to Talk *(1982), Dillard continues this theme as she provides insights that challenge readers to be open and mindful of the relationship between their own lives and that of nature and its creatures.*

A weasel is wild. Who knows what he thinks? He sleeps in his underground den, his tail draped over his nose. Sometimes he lives in his den for two days without leaving. Outside, he stalks rabbits, mice, muskrats, and birds, killing more bodies than he can eat warm, and often dragging the carcasses home. Obedient to instinct, he bites his prey at the neck, either splitting the jugular vein at the throat or crunching the brain at the base of the skull, and he does not let go. One naturalist refused to kill a weasel who was socketed into his hand deeply as a rattlesnake. The man could in no way pry the tiny weasel off, and he had to walk half a mile to water, the weasel dangling from his palm, and soak him off like a stubborn label.

And once, says Ernest Thompson Seton[1]—once, a man shot an eagle out of the sky. He examined the eagle and found the dry skull of a weasel fixed by the jaws to his throat. The **supposition**[2] is that the eagle had pounced on the weasel and the weasel swiveled and bit as instinct taught him, tooth to neck, and nearly won. I would have liked to have seen that eagle from the air a few weeks or months before he was shot: was the whole weasel attached to his feathered throat, a fur pendant? Or did the eagle eat what he could reach, gutting the living weasel with his **talons**[3] before his breast, bending his beak, cleaning the beautiful airborne bones?

I have been thinking about weasels because I saw one last week who startled me, and we exchanged a long glance.

Near my house in Virginia is a pond—Hollins Pond. It covers two acres of bottomland near Tinker Creek with six inches of water and six thousand lily pads. There is a fifty-five mph highway at one end of the pond, and a nesting pair of wood ducks at the other. Under every bush is a muskrat hole or a beer can. The far end is an alternating series of fields and woods, fields and woods, threaded everywhere with motorcycle tracks—in whose bare clay wild turtles lay eggs.

One evening last week at sunset, I walked to the pond and sat on a downed log near the shore. I was watching the lily pads at my feet tremble and part over the thrusting path of a carp. A yellow warbler appeared to my right and flew behind me. It caught my eye,

---

[1] Ernest Thompson Seton (1860–1946) was a naturalist writer and illustrator and cofounder of the Boy Scouts of America.

[2] **supposition**—assumption.

[3] **talons**—claws of a bird of prey.

I swiveled around—and the next instant, **inexplicably**,[4] I was looking down at a weasel who was looking up at me.

Weasel! I had never seen one wild before. He was ten inches long, thin as a curve, a muscled ribbon, brown as fruitwood, soft-furred, alert. His face was fierce, small and pointed as a lizard's; he would have made a good arrowhead. There was just a dot of chin, maybe two brown hairs worth, and then the pure white fur began that spread down his underside. He had two black eyes I did not see, anymore than you see a window.

The weasel was stunned into stillness as he was emerging from beneath an enormous shaggy wild-rose bush four feet away. I was stunned into stillness, twisted backward on the tree trunk. Our eyes locked, and someone threw away the key.

Our look was as if two lovers, or deadly enemies, met unexpectedly on an overgrown path when each had been thinking of something else: a clearing blow to the gut. It was also a bright blow to the brain, or a sudden beating of brains, with all the charge and intimate grate of rubbed balloons. It emptied our lungs. It felled the forest, moved the fields, and drained the pond; the world dismantled and tumbled into that black hole of eyes. If you and I looked at each other that way, our skulls would split and drop to our shoulders. But we don't. We keep our skulls.

He disappeared. This was only last week, and already I don't remember what shattered the enchantment. I think I blinked, I think I retrieved my brain from the weasel's brain, and tried to memorize what I was seeing, and the weasel felt the yank of separation, the careening splashdown into real life and the urgent current of instinct. He vanished under the wild rose. I waited motionless, my mind suddenly full of data and my spirit with pleadings, but he didn't return.

---

[4] **inexplicably**—for some reason difficult or impossible to explain.

Please do not tell me about "approach-avoidance conflicts."[5] I tell you I've been in that weasel's brain for sixty seconds, and he was in mine. Brains are private places, muttering through unique and secret tapes—but the weasel and I both plugged into another tape simultaneously, for a sweet and shocking time. Can I help it if it was a blank?

What goes on in his brain the rest of the time? What does a weasel think about? He won't say. His journal is tracks in clay, a spray of feathers, mouse blood and bone: uncollected, unconnected, looseleaf and blown.

I would like to learn, or remember, how to live. I come to Hollins Pond not so much to learn how to live as, frankly, to forget about it. That is, I don't think I can learn from a wild animal how to live in particular—shall I suck warm blood, hold my tail high, walk with my footprints precisely over the prints of my hands?—but I might learn something of mindlessness, something of the purity of living in the physical senses and dignity of living without bias or motive. The weasel lives in necessity and we live in choice, hating necessity and dying at the last **ignobly**[6] in its talons. I would like to live as I should, as the weasel lives as he should. And I suspect that for me the way is like the weasel's: open to time and death painlessly, noticing everything, remembering nothing, choosing the given with a fierce and pointed will.

I missed my chance. I should have gone for the throat. I should have lunged for the streak of white under the weasel's chin and held on, held on through mud and into the wild rose, held on for a dearer life. We could live under the wild rose wild as weasels, mute and uncomprehending. I could very calmly go wild. I could live two days in the den, curled, leaning on mouse fur, sniffing bird bones, blinking, licking, breathing musk, my hair tangled in the roots of grasses. Down is a good place to go, where the mind is

---

[5] "approach-avoidance conflicts"—refers to the psychological term for being drawn and repelled by the same goal.

[6] **ignobly**—without character or purpose.

single. Down is out, out of your ever-loving mind and back to your careless senses. I remember muteness as a prolonged and giddy fast, where every moment is a feast of utterance received. Time and events are merely poured, unremarked, and ingested directly, like blood pulsed into my gut through a jugular vein. Could two live that way? Could two live under the wild rose, and explore by the pond, so that the smooth mind of each is as everywhere present to the other, and as received and as unchallenged, as falling snow?

We could, you know. We can live anyway we want. People take vows of poverty, chastity, and obedience—even of silence—by choice. The thing is to stalk your calling in a certain skilled and supple way, to locate the most tender and live spot and plug into that pulse. This is yielding, not fighting. A weasel doesn't "attack" anything; a weasel lives as he's meant to, yielding at every moment to the perfect freedom of single necessity.

I think it would be well, and proper, and obedient, and pure, to grasp your one necessity, and not let it go, to dangle from it limp wherever it takes you. Then even death, where you're going no matter how you live, cannot you part. Seize it and let it seize you up aloft even, till your eyes burn out and drop; let your musky flesh fall off in shreds, and let your very bones unhinge and scatter, loosened over fields, over fields and woods, lightly, thoughtlessly, from any height at all, from as high as eagles.

QUESTIONS TO CONSIDER

1. How does seeing the weasel help Dillard define herself?

2. What lessons does Dillard believe humans can learn from weasels?

3. What is Dillard saying in the last paragraph?

ACKNOWLEDGEMENTS

Texts

18 "Why I Live at the P.O." from *A Curtain of Green And Other Stories*, copyright 1941 and renewed 1969 by Eudora Welty, reprinted by permission of Harcourt, Inc.

35 "When I Was Growing Up" by Nellie Wong from *This Bridge Called My Back: Writings by Radical Women of Color* edited by Cherrie Moraga and Gloria Anzaldua. Reprinted by permission of Nellie Wong.

39 Adapted from "Ruth's Song" from *Outrageous Acts And Everyday Rebellions* by Gloria Steinem, © 1983 by Gloria Steinem, 1984 by East Toledo Productions, Inc. Reprinted by permission of Henry Holt and Company, LLC.

56 From *Breath, Eyes, Memory* by Edwidge Danticat. Copyright © 1994 by Edwidge Danticat. Reprinted with permission of Soho Press, NY.

65 "La Gringuita: On Losing a Native Language" by Julia Alvarez. Copyright © 1982, 1998 by Julia Alvarez . Published in *Something To Declare*, Algonquin Books of Chapel Hill, 1998. Reprinted by permission of Susan Bergholz Literary Services, New York. All rights reserved.

86 "Movin' and Steppin'" by Akasha (Gloria) Hull from *Healing Heart: Poems 1973–1988* (New York: Kitchen Table: Women of Color Press). Copyright © 1989 by Gloria T. Hull. Used by permission of the author.

95 "General Review of the Sex Situation", copyright 1926, renewed © 1954 by Dorothy Parker, from *The Portable Dorothy Parker* by Dorothy Parker. Used by permission of Viking Penguin, a division of Penguin Putnam Inc.

108 From *Two or Three Things I Know For Sure* by Dorothy Allison, copyright © 1995 by Dorothy Allison. Used by permission of Dutton, a division of Penguin Putnam Inc.

114 "The Water Faucet Vision" by Gish Jen. Copyright © 1987 by Gish Jen. First published in *Nimrod*. Reprinted by permission of the author.

136 Excerpt from *A Room of One's Own* by Virginia Woolf, copyright 1929 by Harcourt, Inc. and renewed 1957 by Leonard Woolf, reprinted by permission of the publisher.

142 From *The Feminine Mystique* by Betty Friedan. Copyright © 1983, 1974, 1973, 1963 by Betty Friedan. Reprinted by permission of W. W. Norton & Company, Inc.

152 "NOW Bill of Rights" *National Organization of Women*, Adapted by NOW at their First National Conference, Washington DC, 1967. Reprinted by permission of NOW.

Photos

84 Courtesy of Knopf.

182 Underwood & Underwood/CORBIS.

183, 184 *top,* **185** CORBIS.

181, 186, 187 *top,* **192** Bettmann/CORBIS.

187 *bottom* FPG International.

189 Ricardo Watson/Archive Photos.

190 *top,* **192** AP/Wide World Photos.

190–191 Joe Traver/Liaison Agency.

Every effort has been made to secure complete rights and permissions for each selection presented herein. Updated acknowledgements, if needed, will appear in subsequent printings.

Index